HOW TO PARE FOR LEGE

HOW TO PREPARE FOR COLLEGE

Marjorie Eberts
Margaret Gisler

Printed on recyclable paper

VGM Career Horizons
a division of *NTC Publishing Group*
Lincolnwood, Illinois USA

Library of Congress Cataloging-in-Publication Data

Eberts, Marjorie.
  How to prepare for college : Marjorie Eberts, Margaret Gisler.

      p.   cm.
  Includes bibliographical references.
  ISBN 0-8442-6665-5 : $7.95
  1. Universities and colleges—Admission. 2. Study, Methods of.
3. Education. Secondary. I. Gisler, Margaret. II. Title.
LB2351.E24   1989
378.1'056'0973—dc20   89-39301
                                                              CIP

1994 Printing

Published by VGM Career Horizons, a division of NTC Publishing Group.
© 1990 by NTC Publishing Group, 4255 West Touhy Avenue,
Lincolnwood (Chicago), Illinois 60646-1975 U.S.A.

  4 5 6 7 8 9 VP 9 8 7 6 5 4 3

About the Authors

Marjorie Eberts and Margaret Gisler have been writing professionally for ten years. They are prolific free-lance authors with over forty books in print. Their writing is usually in the field of education. The two authors have written textbooks, beginning readers, and study skills books for schoolchildren. They have also written a speech book for young adults and three volumes on the history of an army facility.

Besides writing books, the two authors have a syndicated education column, "Dear Teacher," which appears in newspapers throughout the country. The column gives parents advice on how to guide their children successfully through school. Eberts and Gisler also give advice on educational issues to parents with a weekly television spot.

Eberts is a graduate of Stanford University, and Gisler is a graduate of Ball State and Butler Universities. Both received their specialist degrees in education from Butler University. The two authors are also former teachers with over twenty years of teaching experience between them. Eberts is married and the mother of two children. Gisler is married and the mother of four children.

Acknowledgments

Steve Bushouse, Butler University

Dave Busse, Macalester College

Reid Carpenter, University of Minnesota, Twin Cities

Fred Chandler, Carmel High School, Carmel, Indiana

Martha Eberts, Compass Syndicate Corporation

Dr. Patricia A. Farrant, American College Testing

Maria Patricia Gisler, Compass Syndicate Corporation

Dr. Leonard Gottfried, Purdue University

Paul Thiboutot, Carleton College

To Tricia, Ann, Mark, and David Gisler who are now preparing for college and to Martha and Ken Eberts who prepared diligently and were admitted to college.

Contents

Improving Your Reading   69

Improving Your Basic Skills   89

Becoming an Expert Test Taker   113

School Is More Than Books   124

Organizing the College Admissions Process   130

Taking the College Admissions Tests   153

HOW TO SUCCEED IN HIGH SCHOOL

Section I

Success in College Begins in High School

1

Many students don't realize that their high school years are a preview of what college will be like. There are many similarities between high school and college. In college, students will take notes in class, do homework, study for tests, write term papers, and take final examinations just like they do in high school. They will also participate in extracurricular activities and have part-time jobs. Almost anything that students do in high school prepares them for college.

The more successfully students handle their high school years, the more ready they will be for college. For example, students who have written several term papers in high school will not be overwhelmed when faced with their first term paper assignment in college. Furthermore, students who have learned how to take lecture notes in high school will feel comfortable in college classes where lecturing is often the major method of instruction. They will know how to listen for and write down what is important.

A successful college experience depends on more than a student's academic skills. Students who have learned how to divide their time between schoolwork, extracurricular activities, jobs, and social demands in high school will know how to handle the many conflicting demands on their time at college. Students who have set and achieved goals during their high school years will find it easy to set goals for themselves in college. In the same way, students who have been thinking about possible career choices while they were in high school will find career decisions much simpler to make in college. Finally, students who carefully plan their high school curriculum will find it easier to be admitted to college. In this chapter you will find out something about the steps you need to take while you are in high school in order to prepare yourself for college.

Getting the Most Out of Yourself

You can drift through high school never setting goals, never feeling motivated to do a good job, and never thinking about how you could improve yourself. If you do this, you will not get all you can out of your high school years nor will you have acquired the necessary habits to be successful in college.

Setting long-term goals

You need to know where you are going in the future when you are in high school. You don't have to know exactly what you would like to do, but you should have some idea. Long-term goals will give you direction and motivate you to accomplish the tasks that are essential for you to succeed in high school. For example, students who are thinking about becoming lawyers or actors will want to do well in a speech class because they realize how much the class could help them in the future. On the other hand, students who see the speech class as just a graduation requirement may not be as motivated to do well in the class.

You can daydream about your long-term goals. It can even be motivating to imagine what it would be like to be in college or following a certain career path. Do remember that dreams are wishes, and wishes don't always come true.

Can you answer the following questions with a "yes"?

- Are you planning to attend college?
- Have you thought about what career you would like to pursue?

If you answered "Yes" to both questions, then you have begun to develop long-term goals that will influence much of what you do in high school. For example, if you are planning to attend college, your high school classes will be chosen with that goal in mind. Just as if you are thinking of a career as a newspaper reporter, you will probably want to work on the school newspaper.

Setting short-term goals

Having long-term career goals helps you set many of your short-term goals. These are the goals that can be accomplished within a week or a few months. It takes years to accomplish the long-term goal of becoming an astronaut—a goal that requires college and additional years of training. But along the way, becoming an astronaut also requires accomplishing such short-term goals as making the honor roll, passing next week's test in chemistry, and doing tomorrow's calculus problems correctly.

In order to be admitted to college, most students will need to accomplish the majority of the following short-term goals. Check those goals that you have accomplished:

_____ Learned what several colleges are like.
_____ Researched what high school courses are required for college entrance.
_____ Prepared for college entrance tests.
_____ Received a satisfactory score on the ACT or the SAT.

Goals need to be specific. Long-term goals can be a bit fuzzy, but short-term goals need to be quite specific. While it is admirable to have the goal of becoming a better student during the fall semester, such a goal is so broad that it is difficult to achieve. The goal of spending two hours on your studies each evening is more specific and should help you become a better student.

Goals need to be achievable. When you set goals, you also need to make sure that they are achievable. The goal of receiving an A on the biology final is quite realistic if you have been doing good work in the class. However, if you haven't studied biology very seriously during the school year and have been getting Ds in the subject on all your report cards, such a goal would be very difficult to achieve.

Which goals are achievable? If you don't make short-term goals that are both specific and achievable, you will be discouraged by your efforts to meet them. Decide which of the following goals most students could expect to achieve.

_____ Make straight As.

_____ Pass a biology quiz.

_____ Arrive at school on time every day.

_____ Learn how to diagram sentences.

_____ Win a National Merit Scholarship.

Achieving your goals

You are constantly setting short-term goals in order to complete high school successfully and prepare yourself for college and a future career. Both short-term and long-term goals can seem impossible to realize unless they are broken down into manageable steps. You can compare reaching a goal to climbing a ladder. Each step puts you closer to the top and motivates you to continue your climb.

When you write a term paper, you go through a number of steps like the ones illustrated below. You should break down any goal that you wish to reach in the same organized way.

Goal: Complete a term paper

Select topic
Research term paper
Outline term paper
Write rough draft
Revise rough draft
Write final draft
Proofread final draft
Turn in term paper

Goal: Prepare for a College Entrance Test

One goal that almost every high school student has is to do well on the SAT or ACT. List some of the steps that you will take to accomplish this goal.

_____

_____

_____

_____

_____

Remember: It is having a little belief in yourself, setting achievable goals, and working steadily to achieve each one that will help you reach most of your goals.

What Colleges Expect from You

You want to go to college, but in order to go to college you have to be admitted to one. Knowing the four most important characteristics that colleges are looking for in applicants will help you set goals that will give you the qualifications to be admitted to college.

As you read about what counts in being admitted to college, think about colleges that you might attend. Then for each section write down one or more goals that will help you gain admission to a college that interests you. If you are a freshman or sophomore or even a junior, you have time to set and achieve goals that will help you be admitted to college. Even seniors can improve their chances for admission by having an outstanding year.

Your grades. This is probably the most important factor in your admission to college and placement in certain majors. Most colleges have minimum standards that you must meet. The more selective the college is, the higher your grades need to be.

Grade point average required for college admission: _____

My grade point average: _____

Goals: _____

_____

_____

_____

_____

_____

_____

_____

_____

Your test scores. Most colleges will require you to take either the SAT or ACT for admission. In addition, certain minimum scores must usually be attained for admission. Preparation for these tests will help you score better on them.

Test scores required for college admission:

ACT composite score _____ SAT verbal _____

SAT mathematics _____

My test scores: _____

Goals: _____

_____

_____

_____

_____

_____

_____

_____

_____

_____

Your extracurricular activities. The quality of your participation in extracurricular activities rather than the quantity is what colleges are interested in. They would rather see you be a debating or fencing champion than someone who has dabbled in lots of activities and not gained any particular expertise.

My major extracurricular activities: _____

_____

_____

_____

_____

Goals: _____

_____

_____

_____

_____

_____

_____

_____

Your work experience. Colleges are interested in work experience as another dimension of your abilities. It can be a negative factor if working has hurt your grades.

My jobs: _____

_____

_____

_____

Goals: _____

_____

_____

_____

_____

_____

_____

_____

_____

Exploring Possible Career Goals

In order to set long-term career goals, you must know yourself as well as know something about a variety of possible careers. Knowing yourself, in this case, means being aware of what your interests and strengths are. Take a few minutes right now to write down some information about yourself.

A.   List your main interests in life right now.

_____

_____

B.   List the three high school classes you have found most interesting.

_____

_____

_____

C.   List four things that you do unusually well. This could include making friends, concentrating for long periods of time, or solving math problems.

1.   _____

2.   _____

3.   _____

4.   _____

Look over what you have just written, for it will give you clues about what type of career path you may want to follow. Most people who have successful careers have selected ones that involve doing things that interest them and in which they have skills. If you wrote down that you like tennis, swimming, and soccer, enjoyed your biology class, and are unusually skilled in most sports, you might want to consider a career in something like sports medicine or coaching. Write down in the space below some career goals that tie in with what you have discovered about yourself.

Possible Career Goals: _____

_____

_____

_____

_____

_____

_____

_____

_____

_____

_____

Investigating careers

There are thousands of different careers that you could follow, but there simply isn't time to thoroughly investigate more than a few of them. You should limit your investigation to those careers that tie in closest to your interests and abilities. There are a number of things that you can do during high school to find out about a variety of careers. The more information you have, the better the decision you will be able to make.

Participate in school career days. By attending high school career days, you will get an overview of what several careers are like. You will usually find out about such things as education requirements, training, wage scales, and opportunities for advancement.

Talk to your counselors. You don't have to do everything by yourself. Counselors can help you think of things that you may have overlooked. They can also be of considerable assistance in helping you plan the courses that will help you realize your career goals.

Talk to people working in different careers. People who are working in a career can share with you how they got started in that career and what they like and dislike about it. You can't find this type of personal information in a book.

Join career clubs. At your high school and in the community, there are clubs that are devoted to the exploration of careers. These clubs help you meet people working in different careers and may even help you get part-time jobs to sample more closely what a career is like. Some of these clubs are Junior Achievement Inc., National 4-H Council, Boys Clubs of America, Distributive Education Clubs of America, and Future Homemakers of America.

Get a part-time job. If a career as a hospital administrator interests you, try to get a part-time job at a hospital rather than a fast food restaurant. Working in an area can give you a good idea of whether or not you would like it as a career.

Thinking about the future

Once you have found one or more careers that you might like to follow, you should think about the steps you need to take in the years to come in order to follow these careers. Answer the following questions about each career that you are considering:

1. What should I be doing two years from now to prepare myself to follow this career?

_____

_____

_____

_____

_____

_____

_____

_____

_____

_____

_____

2. What should I be doing four years from now to prepare myself to follow this career?

_____

_____

_____

_____

_____

_____

_____

_____

_____

_____

Choosing Your Classes

You know where you are going when you leave home. You have a route and you follow it. If you have any doubts about where you are going, you probably look at a map or ask someone for directions.

When you have the goal of going to college, you have to know the route that will help you accomplish that goal. One part of that route is the classes that you take in high school. If you don't select the right classes, you may find that you are not able to get into the college of your choice. Furthermore, you may find that you have not even taken the classes necessary for high school graduation or essential to preparing yourself for a career that interests you.

Getting the advice you need

Just as it is smart to ask for directions when you are taking a trip into an unfamiliar area, it is smart to ask for advice when you are preparing for college or a career—unfamiliar areas to you. Obviously, your high school counselor should be one of your primary advisors. You will also find that your parents, older brothers and sisters, and friends who are in high school and college can give you very helpful advice.

The time to consult with these advisors is before you even enter high school. Then you will be sure that you have selected a course of study that will meet high school graduation, college entrance, and career requirements. You won't talk to these advisors only once but each year as you make sure that the courses you have selected are the ones that meet your current needs.

Counselors. Your high school counselors are the experts on high school graduation requirements and will know the entrance requirements for most colleges in your state. The counselors will also help you select a class load that is neither too easy nor too difficult.

Parents. Your parents know how you handle demands on your time. They can help you select a class load that will give you sufficient time to study and still have time for jobs, tasks at home, and extracurricular activities.

Older brothers and sisters and friends. These people know what high school is like. They have taken some of the courses that you will be taking. Ask them what these courses were like and what they got out of them. If any of these people are in college, find out what high school courses really helped them in college and what courses they wish that they had taken to prepare for college.

Selecting your high school courses

The courses that you take in high school fall into two groups: required and electives. In the required group are the classes that you must take for high school graduation and college entrance. In the electives group are the classes that you will take for career preparation and your own personal enjoyment.

High school graduation requirements. These requirements are set by the state and your own high school. Complete the required courses chart adding any additional courses, if necessary, in the space provided. Then check off each requirement as you meet it.

Courses Required for High School Graduation								
Required Courses	Ninth Grade		Tenth Grade		Eleventh Grade		Twelfth Grade	
	Required	Completed	Required	Completed	Required	Completed	Required	Completed
English								
Mathematics								
Science								
U.S. History								
Social Studies								
Physical Education								

College entrance requirements. Different colleges have different entrance requirements. The individual college catalogs will tell you exactly what is required. Most colleges will require you to take a program that includes the following courses:

> Four years of English
>
> Three or four years of college preparatory mathematics
>
> Two or three years of laboratory science
>
> At least two years of one foreign language
>
> At least two years of courses in the social sciences

Cautions:

- Colleges do look at the types of courses that you take to meet their requirements. You need to build a strong academic background. Serious courses like world history are preferred over light ones like the history of television.

- Colleges prefer students to take four years of rigorous academic classes. They frown upon admitting students who take easy class loads any one of their four years in high school.

- Some college majors have specific course requirements, so look for this information when you are determining what courses you need to take.

If you know exactly which college you wish to attend, use its entrance requirements to complete the chart below. Otherwise, use the entrance requirements for a state university or a more selective school, depending upon which type of school you think you will be attending. Check off each requirement as you complete it.

You want to start this chart in ninth grade to make sure that you will be able to complete all of the necessary courses for admission to college. You don't want to discover when you are a senior that you have not taken the appropriate courses for admission to the college of your choice.

Courses Required for College Entrance					
Name of Course	Number of Years of Study Required	High School Courses Completed			
		9	10	11	12
English					
Mathematics					
Science					
Social Studies					
Foreign Language					

Career preparation courses. Once you have made a tentative decision about what career or careers you might like to pursue in the future, you should take some classes in those areas. This will help you decide whether you are truly interested in a career area. It will also help you prepare for a career in that area. For example, someone who wants to become an engineer needs to take classes in mathematics and science.

On the chart below write down the courses that you think might help you prepare for the careers that you are considering.

	Career Preparation Courses		
Possible Career	Courses Helpful in Preparing for This Career		
_____	_____	_____	_____
_____	_____	_____	_____
_____	_____	_____	_____
_____	_____	_____	_____

Your four-year plan   By making out a four-year plan of the courses that you will take in high school, you are setting out the route that will lead to your admission to college. Without such a plan, you may overlook taking a course that is necessary for college admission.

Use the information that you have written down in the sections on graduation requirements, college admission requirements, and career preparation courses to complete your four-year plan. No matter what year you are in school right now, you should complete all four years of the plan. Then you should carefully evaluate your plan and make any necessary changes before you complete your registration for classes each year.

Four-Year Plan of Courses	
Ninth Grade	
First Semester (required courses)	Second Semester (required courses)
(elective courses)	(elective courses)

Tenth Grade	
First Semester (required courses)	Second Semester (required courses)
(elective courses)	(elective courses)

Eleventh Grade	
First Semester (required courses)	Second Semester (required courses)
(elective courses)	(elective courses)

Twelfth Grade	
First Semester (required courses)	Second Semester (required courses)
(elective courses)	(elective courses)

Learning How to Study in High School

You have been studying since the first day you walked into school, and the amount of studying that you have to do has probably increased every year. Have you really learned how to study? Studying isn't a natural process like walking, breathing, or eating. It has to be learned. Unfortunately, few schools really teach students how to study. Without this skill, students find learning far more difficult in high school and college than it should be.

Studying takes a lot of time and energy. Most students do not find studying a pleasant activity. You can probably think of hundreds of other things that you would rather do. How often do you do these things instead of studying? To become really interested in studying, you need to tie it closely to accomplishing your goals of going to college and preparing for a career. You need to have a reason for studying.

In this chapter you will learn how to organize your study place and time. You will also learn about the basic study skills that you need to have for high school and college as well as the special skills needed for different courses. Learning how to study now while you are in high school will make both your high school and college years more enjoyable and successful.

How Do Your Study Skills Rate?

Spending hours studying every day does not necessarily mean that you have good study skills. Nor does getting good grades mean that you have good study skills. Find out how your study skills rate by completing the study skills evaluation exercise.

Study Skills Evaluation

Put a check mark in the blank that best describes the way you study.

	Always	Sometimes	Never	

Study place

I _____ _____ _____ study in the same place at home.

I _____ _____ _____ study in the same place at school.

I _____ _____ _____ organize my study area.

I _____ _____ _____ have supplies in my study area.

Study time

I _____ _____ _____ follow a study schedule.

I _____ _____ _____ study every day.

I _____ _____ _____ study for more than one hour every day.

I _____ _____ _____ do my hardest assignments first.

I _____ _____ _____ review after every class.

I _____ _____ _____ review on days when I have no homework.

I _____ _____ _____ schedule a weekly review session.

Basic study skills

I _____ _____ _____ use different study methods for different subjects.

I _____ _____ _____ concentrate when I study.

I _____ _____ _____ have a list of my daily assignments.

I _____ _____ _____ write my future assignments on a calendar.

I _____ _____ _____ use the SQ3R technique when I study.

I _____ _____ _____ use a dictionary when I study.

I _____ _____ _____ take notes when I study.

I _____ _____ _____ get help when I have trouble understanding something.

I _____ _____ _____ use the correct form when writing an outline.

Classroom study skills

I _____ _____ _____ take notes during class time.

I _____ _____ _____ review my class notes.

I _____ _____ _____ listen attentively during class discussions.

I _____ _____ _____ participate actively in class discussions.

I _____ _____ _____ use textbook aids.

I _____ _____ _____ turn in my assignments on time.

Strengths and weaknesses   Look back over the check marks you made in rating your study skills in four different areas. Hopefully, most of your answers were "always" or "sometimes," indicating that you have good study skills. Every "never" answer shows where there is a weakness in your study skills. The area with the most "always" answers is the one where you have the best study skills, while the one with the most "never" answers is your weakest. Keep your "never" answers in mind as you read through this chapter and the next one so that you can find out how to acquire the study skills that you need. The better your study skills are, the more efficiently you will learn.

Improving your study skills

Your study skills cannot be improved overnight, nor can they be improved by setting fuzzy goals. You need to set specific short-term goals in order to acquire the skills that you need. Acquiring skills like keeping a list of assignments, reviewing after every class, and participating actively in class discussions can dramatically improve the way you study. Begin to improve your study skills by selecting three skills where you placed check marks under "never," and make it your goal to acquire those skills within four weeks. Keep track of your progress on the following chart:

Today's date _____

Study goal # one _____

_____

_____

_____

_____

Date in four weeks _____

Improvement noted _____

_____

_____

_____

Today's date _____

Study goal # two _____

_____

_____

_____

_____

Date in four weeks _____

Improvement noted _____

_____

_____

_____

_____

Today's date _____

Study goal # three _____

_____

_____

_____

_____

Date in four weeks _____

Improvement noted _____

_____

_____

_____

_____

Finding Out How You Learn   An important part of knowing how to study lies in knowing how you best learn. Did you know that everyone does not learn in the same way? Everyone has his or her own distinct learning style. Your learning style is different from your best friend's and even your brother's and sister's. You need to find out what your own personal learning style is so that you can use that style when you are studying.

Your Learning Style Questionnaire

Circle the answers that best complete the following statements.

1. I remember things best when I study
   a. early in the morning.
   b. at school.
   c. in the afternoon after school.
   d. after dinner.
   e. late at night.

2. I study best when I am
   a. with one friend.
   b. alone.
   c. with a study group.
   d. with the teacher.
   e. sometimes alone and sometimes with a friend.
   f. with an adult.

3. The things I learn best, I learn by
   a. reading them.
   b. writing them down.
   c. hearing them.
   d. reading and writing them.
   e. reading and hearing them.
   f. writing and hearing them.
   g. a combination of reading, writing, and hearing them.

4. The things I learn best I learn through
   a. my eyes.
   b. my ears.
   c. my touch.
   d. a combination of _____.

5. I study best when the lighting is
   a. strong.
   b. of average intensity.

   c. very low.

   d. sunlight.

6. I concentrate best when my study area is

   a. hot.

   b. warm.

   c. cool.

   d. so cold that I need to wear a sweater.

7. I study best

   a. sitting in a comfortable chair.

   b. sitting at a desk.

   c. sitting or lying on the floor.

   d. sitting or lying on a bed.

8. I concentrate best when

   a. there is no noise.

   b. it is relatively quiet.

   c. there is light background noise.

   d. there is considerable noise.

   e. the television is on.

9. When I study best, I need

   a. to eat as I study.

   b. to have just eaten.

   c. to be hungry.

   d. to chew gum.

   e. to drink water or soda.

   f. to have no food or beverage.

10. When I study best, I

   a. study for a long period of time.

   b. study for at least one hour.

   c. study at least 30 minutes at a time.

   d. study at least 15 minutes at a time.

Your personal learning profile

Look back over the answers that you circled. Now use these answers to create your own learning profile. This profile will give you a picture of how you learn best.

LEARNING PROFILE
Environmental Needs (5, 6, 7, 8)

I study best when

the lighting is _____,

the temperature is _____,

the sound level is _____,

and the place I am working at is _____.

Social Needs (2)

I study best when I am _____.

Sensory Needs (3, 4)

I study best when the sense(s) I mainly use is (are) my

_____ and I learn by _____.

Physical Needs (1, 9, 10)

I study best when my study time is _____,

the amount of time I study is _____,

and the food or drink I am consuming is _____

_____.

Setting Up a Study Place

You don't need a fancy study area, but you do need to establish one place for doing most of your studying. This place does not have to be a soundproof cell. However, it shouldn't be a recreational area either. It does not matter if you select a study place for yourself at home, at school, or in a library as long as you usually study in the same place. The importance of studying in the same place is that you don't waste time and energy adjusting to new sights, sounds, smells, and distractions every time you study.

If you don't already have a study area, select one now. Try to select an area that is away from a lot of traffic and distractions. It should be a place where you honestly believe you will be able to get your studying done.

I plan to do most of my studying in _____

_____.

Choosing the best conditions

Now that you have selected your study area, you will need to make sure that the area meets all the environmental conditions under which you learn best. You may find it helpful to go back and look at your learning profile.

Sound level. Noise can distract you from studying. Even background noise can cause you problems if you are not used to the noise. Try to lower the volume if you like to study with loud music blasting in your ears, for research does show it will disrupt your studying. However, if you find that soft music helps drown out other interferring noises in your study area or that it helps to keep your mind focused, make sure you have it.

Lights. When you are checking the lighting in your study area, take into account the direction from which any daylight or artificial light will fall. You want to avoid having a glare. The best way to avoid a glare is to have the main light source come from the side. Try to have good lighting over your books at all times. You should know that very bright or dim light, even if you prefer it, can cause eye strain.

Temperature. The temperature of your study area will affect your learning. If it is too hot, you may find it easy to fall asleep. On the other hand, if it is too cold, you will find it hard to concentrate on anything except getting warm. The ideal temperature for a study area is usually approximately 70°F (21°C).

Comfort. Your comfort as you study is important. Make sure that your study area has whatever you need to study best—a comfortable chair, a desk and chair, or a bed.

Air circulation. Is the air circulation good in the place you have chosen as your study area? You need a good supply of oxygen to be mentally and physically alert as you study.

Having a good work surface

Your study area needs a place where you can do written assignments. Even if you do most of your studying while lying on the floor, you still need to have a good work surface in your study area. It should be placed in a spot where distractions won't interrupt your studying—for example, against a wall is better than in front of a window.

The work surface should be at a height that will let you do your work in a comfortable position. Your chair should provide good support for your lower back and shoulders. A chair without this support will cause you to tire quickly.

The top of the work surface should be large enough to hold everything that you will need while studying. Most students know that they need their books and notebooks but forget they may need additional things like a calculator, typewriter, or computer. List the things that you will need on your work surface.

_____ _____ _____

_____ _____ _____

You should also have a storage area near your work surface so that you can reach all your supplies without getting up and down like a yo-yo.

Equipping your study area

You need to make sure that your study area has all the supplies that you need before you begin using it. Otherwise, you will be constantly interrupting your study sessions to find the supplies you need. Check over the supply list below. Add any additional items that you feel you need to complete your list.

Basic Supplies	Have	Need to Have
atlas	_____	_____
calculator	_____	_____

colored paper	_____	_____
colored pencils	_____	_____
compass	_____	_____
computer	_____	_____
crayons	_____	_____
dictionary	_____	_____
encyclopedias	_____	_____
erasers	_____	_____
felt tip pens	_____	_____
folders	_____	_____
glue	_____	_____
graph paper	_____	_____
highlighter pens	_____	_____
index cards	_____	_____
marking pens	_____	_____
paper	_____	_____
pencils	_____	_____
pencil sharpener	_____	_____
rubber bands	_____	_____
ruler	_____	_____
scissors	_____	_____
scotch tape	_____	_____
scrap paper	_____	_____
stapler	_____	_____
stencils	_____	_____
thesaurus	_____	_____
typewriter	_____	_____
typing paper	_____	_____
_____	_____	_____
_____	_____	_____
_____	_____	_____
_____	_____	_____

Checking your study area

Go back to your learning profile once more and make sure that your study area meets your environmental needs for learning. Look around your study area and remove any objects that you could find distracting. You should also take away other items that are not necessary and that cause clutter. Check to see if you have purchased all the supplies that you need and that they have been stored close to your work surface.

Using your study area

As you start to use your study area, you will find things that need to be changed. You will also find there are distractions that annoy you. It could be a sprinkler hitting against your home or a constantly ringing telephone. Make a list of these distractions and then try to think of the best way to eliminate each one as quickly as possible.

No study area, even your own, can be perfect. If you follow the guidelines in this section in setting up your study area, you should have a place where you will be able to work faster, feel more alert, and have more productive study time.

Remember, your physical health also plays an important part in your studying. So you should try to get enough sleep and eat three well-balanced meals a day. Being hungry or tired can affect the quality of your study time even if all the environmental conditions are close to perfect for you.

Finding Time to Study

You have set up your own study place, and now you need to find the time to use it. Did you know that there are 168 hours in a week? For quite a few of those hours you are busy eating, sleeping, and going to school. What are you doing with the rest of your time? You control much of what you do with this time. How much of it are you using for studying and activities that really matter to you?

Your time is one of your most important resources. You should know how you are using it and plan to use it productively. Fill out the weekly time chart so you can see at a glance where all your hours are going. Describe your activities every half hour from the time you get up until you go to bed. Be specific. Tell exactly what you were doing—on the telephone, watching television, reading.

Weekly Time Chart of Activities

Time	Activity						
	Monday	Tuesday	Wednesday	Thursday	Friday	Saturday	Sunday
6:30–7:00							
7:00–7:30							
7:00–7:30							
7:30–8:00							
8:00–8:30							
8:30–9:00							
9:00–9:30							
10:00–10:30							
10:30–11:00							
11:00 11:30							
12:00–12:30							

(cont.)

Time	Activity						
	Monday	Tuesday	Wednesday	Thursday	Friday	Saturday	Sunday
12:30–1:00							
1:00–1:30							
1:30–2:00							
2:00–2:30							
2:30–3:00							
3:00–3:30							
3:30–4:00							
4:00–4:30							
4:30–5:00							
5:00–5:30							
5:30–6:00							
6:00–6:30							

Time	Activity						
	Monday	Tuesday	Wednesday	Thursday	Friday	Saturday	Sunday
6:30–7:00							
7:00–7:30							
7:30–8:00							
8:00–8:30							
8:30–9:00							
9:00–9:30							
9:30–10:00							
10:00–10:30							
10:30–11:00							
11:00–11:30							
11:30–12:00							

Analyzing how you spend your time

Look back over your time chart and see how much time you devoted to the following activities so that you will have a better idea of how you spend your time.

Required Activities	Hours Spent on Activity
Time spent at school	_____
Time spent sleeping	_____
Time spent in after-school activities	_____
Time spent eating	_____
Time spent working	_____
Total time spent on required activities	_____

Other Activities

Time spent visiting with friends	_____
Time spent visiting with family	_____
Time spent watching television	_____
Time spent talking on the telephone	_____
Time spent on no particular activity	_____
Time spent studying	_____
Total time spent on other activities	_____

Your time. Were you surprised by how you actually spent your time? Do you think your time was well used? Of course, your study time is important, but so is concentrating on extracurricular activities. Was too much of your time frittered away not doing anything special?

Study time. Are you spending enough time studying? In college, you will be expected to spend at least one hour studying for every hour in class. In high school, you should spend enough time studying to complete all your assignments, to review your schoolwork daily, and to study for quizzes and tests. For most students, this means at least an hour of studying outside of school each day.

Planning more productive use of your time

With a little planning, you can create a schedule that will help you use your time more productively. If you don't have definite times for studying, then you probably will put it off. For example, you may have to do some math problems, but you delay by watching television before dinner, talking on the phone after dinner, fixing a snack, and so on. Then you try to do the problems right before you go to bed or tell yourself that you will get up in the morning and do them.

Having a definite time to study each day—not necessarily the same time—gives you the organized approach to studying that you will need for college. In college, no one will tell you when to study—it is completely up to you. Learning to arrange your study time in high school makes it much easier to handle the greater freedom you will have in college. Just as you need to schedule your study time, you need to schedule time for activities that are important to you. You need time for tennis lessons, practicing the piano, and volunteer activities.

Do you realize that good time management will:

- save you time
- give you more time to relax
- give you time to concentrate on your interests
- give you time to do more things
- improve your study habits
- give a sense of purpose to your days

Can you really afford to pass up the benefits of scheduling your time?

Beginning your time schedule. Look for the pitfalls in how you have been spending your time, according to the weekly time chart you just made, before starting to create a time schedule. Ask yourself the following questions:

1. Did you plan your study time in advance?   yes   no
2. Did you study before class?   yes   no
3. Did you study right after class?   yes   no
4. Did social activities interrupt your studying?   yes   no
5. Did you build in regular time for reviewing?   yes   no
6. Did you provide time for extra projects?   yes   no
7. Did you have to cram?   yes   no
8. Did you have time to relax?   yes   no
9. Did you have free time?   yes   no
10. Did you get enough sleep?   yes   no

Every "no" answer is a pitfall you will want to avoid when creating your time schedule.

Basic guidelines. It does not matter what year you are in high school, there are some basic guidelines you will need to follow in planning your time schedule:

- Use your schedule to meet your goals.
- Consider your study priorities. (Which classes need more time?)
- Plan study times before or right after classes when possible.
- Plan for emergencies.
- Schedule adequate time for study—neither too little nor too much.
- Build in time for review.
- Block off time for projects.
- Schedule sufficient free time.
- Build in flexibility.

Some time considerations. Keep in mind that you will remember more after five one-hour study sessions spread over a week than one five-hour cram session. You should try to study every major subject at least a half hour a day. On weekends, you can schedule time for classes that are giving you problems.

There is no one time of day when everyone should study. When you should schedule your study time depends on your learning style. Most people have a time when they are functioning at their best—that is the ideal time for scheduling as much of your studying as possible.

Your study schedule. Use the following chart to make your personal study schedule. Keep all the guidelines and time considerations in mind as you make your schedule. Write down all your scheduled activities, then allot time for studying and special activities. The remaining time should be free time. You don't want to schedule every minute of your life.

Personal Study Schedule

Hours	Monday	Tuesday	Wednesday	Thursday	Friday	Saturday	Sunday
6:00–6:30							
6:30–7:00							
7:00–7:30							
7:30–8:00							
8:00–8:30							
8:30–9:00							
9:00–9:30							
9:30–10:00							
10:00–10:30							
10:30–11:00							
11:00–11:30							
11:30–12:00							

Hours	Monday	Tuesday	Wednesday	Thursday	Friday	Saturday	Sunday
12:00–12:30							
12:30–1:00							
1:00–1:30							
1:30–2:00							
2:00–2:30							
2:30–3:00							
3:00–3:30							
3:30–4:00							
4:00–4:30							
4:30–5:00							
5:00–5:30							
5:30–6:00							

(cont.)

Hours	Monday	Tuesday	Wednesday	Thursday	Friday	Saturday	Sunday
6:00–6:30							
6:30–7:00							
7:00–7:30							
7:30–8:00							
8:00–8:30							
8:30–9:00							
9:00–9:30							
9:30–10:00							
10:00–10:30							
10:30–11:00							
11:00–11:30							
11:30–12:00							

Following your schedule. A study schedule has no value unless you follow it. If your schedule seems impossible to follow, you may be scheduling too much of your time. Keep adjusting your schedule until you get one that really works for you. You will approach your schoolwork with far more confidence when you know that you have scheduled your time in such a way that you will be able to handle whatever needs to be done.

Aids for More Efficient Studying

Good students are rarely puzzled about when an assignment is due, what the day's homework is, or where their study guide for a test is. They handle these day-to-day needs by using aids that make their studying far easier and more efficient. They also know how to use such aids as computers, calculators, encyclopedias, dictionaries, and flash cards.

Calendar. Every student needs a calendar with sufficient space to write down future assignments and events. You may have a project due in three weeks and believe you have ample time in which to get it done. However, you may also have several other assignments due during that time period and some important social engagements. Time passes swiftly, and you may forget all your obligations and have to burn the midnight oil in order to get the project turned in on time. By using a calendar, you can plan for future events. You know when to start preparing for tests and when to finish different parts of a project. You should have a calendar in your study area and should thumb through it at the start of every study session. A calendar banishes unpleasant surprises.

Assignment notebook. You need to have a daily record of your assignments for every class. Take an assignment notebook to each class and write down the details of every assignment as well as the dates for quizzes and tests and the deadlines for turning in papers and projects. Check your assignment notebook before you leave school each day so that you take home all the books and materials that you will need. Then make sure that you always write all the dates and deadlines from your assignment notebook down on your calendar and also on your weekly time schedule.

Daily "do" list. A list of what must be done each day will help you make sure that nothing is forgotten like an appointment with a counselor or a meeting after school. Check your calendar when you make up your list for each day.

Notebooks and folders. Every day you complete papers, do study guides, and get quizzes and tests returned to you. Develop a system for keeping the papers for each class together by using separate folders or notebooks with sections for each class. Store the papers you are not currently using but will need later on in folders in your study area.

Computer. If you are lucky enough to have a computer, learn to use it. It makes writing papers a breeze because it is so easy to make revisions. Most colleges have computers or computer terminals in libraries and dormitories. You will want to use a computer to write all your papers when you are in college.

You can also use commercial programs to improve a variety of your skills such as spelling and mathematics. You can even prepare for the SAT on the computer. Computer assisted instruction (CAI) can actually teach you in a step-by-step approach such subjects as biology and history. The program keeps working with you until you have mastered the subject matter and at the end of each lesson judges your performance.

Calculator. High school students use calculators in their advanced math and science classes. You will also need to use a calculator in college in classes like economics, statistics, and psychology. Use a calculator to eliminate your fears about accuracy in all of your calculations.

Encyclopedias. When you want to know the who, what, when, where, how, or why of almost anything in a very short time, the encyclopedia is the study aid that will give you a quick overview.

Dictionary. The dictionary must be used every time you have the slightest doubt about how a word is spelled or what it means.

Flash cards. When you have to memorize anything—from definitions to chemical formulas to words in a foreign language—flash cards are what you should use. They are also extremely helpful to use in preparing for all kinds of tests.

Study Techniques You Need to Know

To do well in high school and prepare yourself for college, it isn't enough to know how you learn and to be a well-organized student. You have to know how to study. This means knowing how to get the most out of your textbooks and being able to outline, take notes, and underline. You simply must master these basic study techniques plus understand the importance of regular review of all your work.

How to use a textbook

For both high school and college students, textbooks contain the information that most teachers expect them to learn. Fortunately, textbooks are usually organized in a way that helps you learn information easily. What is important is clearly emphasized.

You must learn all the words in word lists at the start or end of a chapter as well as all the words in boldface or italic type. Once you know what these words mean, you have a clear understanding of the key concepts of a chapter. The headings give you a preview of each section so you always know what you are supposed to learn, while the summaries at the end of a chapter tell you what you should have learned. If you thoroughly understand the summary of a chapter, then you probably have mastered what you need to know in a chapter. It is easy to check your mastery. All you have to do is to complete the exercises at the end of a chapter. As you study a chapter you should look at all the pictures, illustrations, and charts, for they will make the meaning of what is said much clearer.

Knowing what is in the different parts of a textbook helps you use it. The table of contents in the front of the book will give you general information about what is covered in each chapter. The glossary is really a small dictionary of all the important terms used in the book. It gives you the pronunciation and definition of many of the technical words that you will not know. The index gives you an alphabetical list of the topics covered in the textbook. And if you are looking for additional reading, you will usually find a bibliography in most textbooks that will provide you with a reading list.

Textbook aids. When you are having difficulty in understanding a textbook, read the introduction carefully to find out if the publisher offers aids like study guides, workbooks, and extra problem sets. You will find these aids to be very helpful.

SQ3R—one way to study a textbook

One of the best ways to learn the material in a textbook is by using the SQ3R study technique. Your third or fourth grade teacher might have taught this technique to you, and if so, you should have been using it ever since then with every textbook that you studied. The letters in SQ3R stand for the steps that you follow in studying a textbook.

S stands for survey. You begin by surveying a reading assignment. This means looking at all the headings and subheadings in the assigned material. This is the material that stands out in different type. Once you have a general picture of what you are to study, you go on to the next step.

Q stands for question. Make a question for the first heading. You are asking yourself what you are going to learn in that section. The question gives you a challenge— a reason to continue studying. You can also make questions for subheadings. Keep your questions for future study sessions. Make sure you leave room between each question for your answers.

R stands for read. After you have written your first question, you read the material under the heading thoroughly and carefully to find the answer. Don't overlook reading captions under pictures and all illustrations. Do take the time to look up any word that you do not know as you are reading.

R stands for recite. As soon as you have read and found the answer to your question, recite the answer out loud without looking at the text. For additional reinforcement, write the answer to your question. Then follow the same steps for the remaining headings in your assignment.

R stands for review. Before putting your textbook away, review all the material you have studied during your study session. To review, you must skim over the headings again, recite the important ideas under each heading, and answer the questions you wrote. If there are any questions that you can't answer, you need to reread the material as well as your answers. Then do any exercises that are included in the assigned material.

SQ3R's benefits. At first, you may find the SQ3R technique very time consuming. However, if you repeat the review step a few hours after completing it the first time and every few days after that, you will find that you have really learned the material. Studying for a test over the material will not need to be any more than the last step of SQ3R. The more you use SQ3R, the quicker you will be able to use it and the more convinced you will become of the benefits of this study technique. Try it now over just this section on SQ3R. Reread the headings to survey the section. Then answer this question: how do you use SQ3R to study a textbook?

Outlining—another way to study a textbook

Textbooks are written from outlines. The main ideas of the outline are the major headings of the textbook, and the subheadings represent the supporting details. Outlining helps you group ideas together in such a way that you can clearly see the relationships between the main ideas and the details that support them. When you outline a textbook, you are discovering what the author or authors thought was important. At the same time, you are creating a tool that you can use in preparing for tests.

You must follow a standard form when writing an outline. The major rule is that each division of an outline must have at least two subdivisions. Study the following outline to see if you really know how to organize one.

Title

    I. Main idea

        A. Subtopic

            1. Major detail

                (a) Minor detail

                    (1) Item supporting minor detail

                    (2) Item supporting minor detail

                (b) Minor detail

            2. Major detail

        B. Subtopic

    II. Main idea

        A. Subtopic

        B. Subtopic

Testing your outlining skills. See if you can complete this outline of the first few pages of this chapter.

Learning How to Study in High School

  I. How do your study skills rate?

    A. Strengths and weaknesses in your study skills

    B. _____

       _____

 II. _____

     _____

    A. Your learning style questionnaire

    B. _____

       _____

III. Setting up a place to study

A. _____

_____

1. sound levels

2. lights

3. _____

4. _____

5. _____

B. Having a good work surface

Avoid excessive detail. You can make outlines as detailed as you want, but be careful not to make your outline so detailed that you are almost rewriting the textbook.

Underlining and studying

College students will often underline their textbooks and notebooks. It is difficult for high school students to get much experience in underlining since they can underline only in books or notebooks that they own. Underlining, however, can help you when you review class notes, SQ3R notes, outlines, and study guides. Underline the key words, dates, definitions, and names that you need to remember. Just be discreet. If you get carried away with your underling, you will defeat the purpose of this technique. Underlining is especially useful after you have reviewed your SQ3R notes a few times. By then you will know most of the material so you can just underline the high points you need to remember—making reviewing a much simpler task. Practice underlining now by rereading and underlining this section on underlining and studying.

Taking notes

Taking notes while you are studying a textbook will reinforce what you are learning. In fact, the more senses that students use when studying, the easier it is to learn. Note taking involves writing down what you want to remember from what you are reading. Just don't make the mistake of writing out the whole textbook. You need to be very selective about what you write down.

College students often take notes right in the margins of their textbooks. You may find it helpful to take notes on binder paper so that you can rearrange your notes or insert any additional notes or information in your binder or notebook. Besides making frequent use of abbreviations in their notes, some students develop their own form of shorthand so they don't have to write as much. Try your hand at shortening the following common words. Just don't make your shorthand system so complicated that when you look back over your notes, you cannot interpret them.

vocabulary _____   encyclopedia _____

high school _____   textbook _____

homework _____   assignment _____

Reviewing—a most important study technique

You know the importance of studying. You also must realize the importance of regularly reviewing your work in every class. Reviewing helps you remember what you studied today, yesterday, and last month. It is very easy to forget material that you have just studied. You need to review your notes, outlines, study guides, and any other materials you have for each class frequently. Your first review session should ideally take place shortly after you have learned new material. Then you should review it a few days later. At least once a week you should spend time reviewing so that you can keep the total picture in your mind of what you are learning in each class. Your review periods do not need to be long—in fact, fifteen minutes should be sufficient for each subject.

Suggestions for Studying Different Subjects

Considering the number of years that you have been in school already, no one needs to tell you that every subject in school deals with different kinds of information. However, even students, as experienced as you are, often don't realize that each subject needs to be studied differently. You will find school quite difficult if you are studying English the same way you study science. It is somewhat like working on your golf swing in your physical education class and expecting it to improve your bowling score.

Not only does every subject have to be studied in a different way, every subject has its own vocabulary. Match the following words to the subjects where you are most likely to find them.

Subject Words   **Subject**

_____ numerator   a. social studies

_____ impeachment   b. English

_____ magma   c. science

_____ modifier   d. mathematics

_____ treaty

_____ diameter

_____ hyphen

Studying mathematics Mathematics is a subject where you are constantly building on what you have learned earlier. You simply can't do complicated multiplication problems if your addition is shaky. Since each day's work is important, you must get in the habit of always doing your daily work. Furthermore, at the first sign of trouble you should seek help so you won't have a weak link in your math skills. You need to get a solid math background in high school because you will be using math in such college courses as psychology, economics, and almost every science class.

Math classes usually work in this way. A new topic is introduced in the textbook, your teacher does some sample problems, and then you are assigned some problems.

Preparation. To prepare yourself to do your assignment you should follow these steps:

- Take notes on your teacher's explanations.
- Copy each problem that your teacher puts on the board in your math notebook.
- Read the textbook and redo the sample problems.
- Review all your notes before beginning an assignment.

- Try to do your math assignments as soon after your math class as possible so what you learned in class will still be fresh in your mind.

Handling assignments. Use the following techniques while doing your assignments:

- Write numbers as neatly as you can.
- Get in the habit of using estimation to determine if your answers seem correct.
- If you run into difficulty with a problem, try substituting smaller numbers and then see if you can solve the problem.
- Read all story problems more than once. The last sentence will usually tell you what you are trying to find out. Draw diagrams when appropriate.
- Check your answers with answers in the textbook when possible.

Additional hints:

- Keep all old quizzes and tests to use in preparing for chapter and final tests. The test problems are likely to be similar. Prepare by redoing the problems.
- Learn to be proficient with the calculator.

Studying social studies   It simply isn't possible to call reading a section or chapter in a social studies textbook studying. Studying means being actively involved with what you are trying to learn. Use the SQ3R technique, outline the material, or take notes whenever you have an assignment in your social studies textbook.

To remember which events occurred before or after other events, get in the habit of creating timelines. And to memorize names, terms, and dates, use flash cards.

Studying science   You must approach your study of science in a very organized way. All textbook notes, class notes, and study guides for a chapter must be kept together as you will need to look at them when preparing for labs and studying for tests.

In science classes, you have to learn a great number of new words as well as formulas. Flash cards can be very helpful in doing this. As in social studies, you need to use SQ3R, outline, or take notes in order to learn the textbook material. It also helps to preview a section in a textbook before it is discussed in class so that you will feel more at home with the new material.

Because a lot of difficult material is covered in science, you will need to study any science course daily and to review frequently. You cannot afford to get behind in science classes because so much material is covered. On lab days, you must know what you are going to do before the session begins in order to fully understand the experiments you are going to do.

Studying a foreign language

Studying a foreign language involves learning three different skills at the same time: speaking, reading, and writing. So whenever you are working on one skill, try to reinforce it by using another at the same time. For example, when you are writing out an exercise, read it aloud at the same time.

It takes years to learn a foreign language. The language that you start learning in high school you may continue studying in college. Therefore you may want to use your high school flash cards and notebooks in college. Start your vocabulary flash cards the first day you enter high school. At the same time start a notebook with sections on grammar and culture. If you use a binder, you can keep adding and rearranging the pages.

Foreign languages are a lot like mathematics since both subjects are cumulative and everything you learn must be remembered. What you learned the first day in high school French you will be using in your junior year in college when you study in France.

Studying English

Most students take English classes during their first year in college. They will also have to take a great number of essay tests during their college years. In order to be ready for college, you should know and be able to apply the rules of English grammar as well as be able to write compositions, term papers, and reports.

During your high school years, concentrate on learning what you don't know about English. Every time you make a mistake in an exercise or have red correction marks on a theme, find out exactly what you did wrong and learn how to correct your error.

Five Important Study Tips

By now you should have selected and set up your own study area. You should also at least be working on your time schedule. The study tips that follow are five important tips that will really make a difference if you follow them.

Study what you don't know. You should never waste time rereading or studying what you already know. Instead, you should make lists of what you don't know and study this material.

Review after every class. Your memory is short. You need to review as soon as possible after every class. This will help to reinforce the material that you have just learned.

Schedule weekly review sessions. You should review what is being covered in each grading period at least once a week. Reviewing strengthens your learning.

Get help fast. Whenever you don't understand something, you should get help immediately. You can talk to the teacher, a classmate, a parent, or a tutor.

Study every day. You need to study at least one hour every day now that you are in high school.

Acing the Classroom Experience 3

Everywhere you turn you are always hearing about the importance of a good education. You know that your high school education is important because it will play an important part in determining where you will go to college and what career you will be able to pursue.

Successful people often say that it was their education that helped them get where they are today. You get your education in many places. However, the major part of your education right now is being acquired in your high school classrooms.

Going to class is important, but it is not enough. In this chapter you will find out how to get the education that you need from the classroom.

Regular Attendance Is Important

It is trite, but true. The only person you are hurting is yourself when you cut class. In order to acquire a good high school education and be really prepared for college, you must attend all your classes regularly. When you miss class, you are missing a major part of your education. You can catch up on missed material in the textbook, but you can never catch up on what was discussed in the classroom. You miss learning your teachers' and other students' feelings on issues. You miss explanations of concepts that go beyond what is said in textbooks. You miss knowing how your feelings and knowledge would have changed if you had been in class. And you also deprive the other students in your classes of your input. Attending class right before a test or near the end of the semester is especially important since teachers tend to stress what is really essential to know at those times.

If you are sick or unable to attend class for a few days, make sure you get all the assignments. But more than that, ask the teacher if you can copy his or her notes or get notes from someone in the class who really records what happened. It also helps to talk to a classmate about what was discussed in class in order to give life to the notes that you have read and copied.

Come Prepared for Your Classes

Many students simply don't realize that being prepared makes a world of difference in what they will learn from a class. Going to class without the supplies you need is rather like trying to play baseball without a glove. You just can't play the game right. Going without your assignments completed can be compared to running a marathon without any preparation. You won't accomplish much.

Having your supplies is important

Have you ever found yourself in geometry class without your protractor or in English without your textbook? You are not alone. The problem of not having what you need for class is a common one for students. It is a simple problem that you can eliminate by putting a checklist on the front of each one of your class notebooks or on the front of your assignment notebook or even on your locker door. Then all you have to do to be perfectly equipped is to look over your checklist before you leave home or your locker for your classes. You may find it helpful to use a checklist like the following one or create a new one that fits your needs better.

Name of class

Have completed assignment

Have textbook

Have notebook

Have workbook or lab manual, if needed

Have sharpened pencils

Have pens

Have other needed supplies

_____

_____

_____

Your assignments need to be completed

Notice that the number one priority on the checklist is to have your assignment completed. What this really means is are you ready to learn? If you haven't done the background reading, your participation in the class discussion will be limited. If you haven't done the written assignment, you will be playing catch-up for the entire class period. Furthermore, the teacher will quickly see you are unprepared for class.

It is important to realize that teachers make assignments for a reason—not just to keep you busy. Assignments give you the opportunity to practice the skills that you are learning in class, especially in English, foreign language, and math classes. They help you develop the skills that you will need in college and your career. Assignments also let you learn new material through your textbooks and prepare you to participate in class discussions. Assignments allow you to complete work that you began in class. Furthermore, they help you review what you have been learning in your classes.

Completing assignments helps you develop the good study habits that you will need in college. Go through the following assignment preparation checklist.

Assignment Preparation Checklist
1. Do you try to do all your assignments at the same time every day?   yes   no

2. Do you keep an assignment notebook?   yes   no

3. Do you review or work ahead on days when you don't have any assigned homework?   yes   no

4. Do you make a list of questions of things that you do not understand in your assignments?   yes   no

5. Do you keep a calendar that shows when future assignments are due?   yes   no

6. Do you get help when you are having trouble with an assignment?   yes   no

If you answered "no" to any of the questions on the checklist, set some goals now to improve those areas and keep a record of your progress on the following chart:

Today's date _____

Assignment preparation goal # one _____

_____

_____

_____

Date in four weeks _____

Improvement noted _____

_____

_____

_____

Today's date _____

Assignment preparation goal # two _____

_____

_____

_____

Date in four weeks _____

Improvement noted _____

_____

_____

_____

Choose a Good Seat
The heading "choose a good seat" may be making you laugh even before you begin to read the reasons why this heading is necessary. First, answer this question: where do you pick to sit in a class when you are given this choice?

1. Do you try to sit in the back of the room? yes no

2. Do you try to sit in the middle of the room? yes no

3. Do you try to sit in the front of the room? yes no

You are on the right track if you answered "yes" to question number three. The very best seats in any classroom are the ones in the front row. By sitting in the front row or as close to the front as possible, you are eliminating many of the distractions that can tear your concentration away from the classwork. You don't have to watch what other students are doing. You can see the teacher and the work that is done on the blackboard. Because you are so visible to the teacher, you will be inclined to concentrate more on the lesson. In addition, you may have a chance for more casual conversation with the teacher.

Many students feel more comfortable and secure sitting further back in a classroom. It requires some courage to sit up front. You will usually be called on more often by the teacher so you will always need to be prepared. You will never have the chance to have a quick nap or even daydream for a few minutes. However, since you are in a class to learn, it makes sense to pick a seat that will give you the best opportunity to learn. If you have never tried sitting in the front of a classroom, try it. You may be surprised to find out that where you sit can make a difference.

Participation Is Essential

By now you should know that what you say in class does make a difference. It is so important that some teachers in high school and even in college give a grade for class participation. But participation is more than winning "brownie" points with your teachers. It is being actively involved in the learning process. If you don't participate, you are rather like a sponge expecting to absorb learning because you are there. To participate, you need to be prepared, which certainly helps you learn. There is also an interesting benefit to participation. By participating in a class you become interested in what you are learning and more eager to study.

Check your classroom participation. Answer the following questions to determine how well you are participating in your classes right now.

1. Do I have a good attendance record?   yes   no
2. Do I pay attention to what is being said?   yes   no
3. Do I take notes on class discussions?   yes   no
4. Am I usually prepared to participate in class discussions?   yes   no
5. Do I answer questions willingly?   yes   no
6. Are my contributions valuable?   yes   no

Any "no" answers indicate areas that you should improve. Since both you and your classmates are enriched when you participate in class discussions, you should set some goals to improve your participation, if necessary.

Today's date _____

Participation goal # one _____

_____

_____

_____

_____

Date in four weeks _____

Improvement noted _____

_____

_____

_____

_____

Today's date _____

Participation goal # two _____

_____

_____

_____

_____

Date in four weeks _____

Improvement noted _____

_____

_____

_____

_____

Preparing to participate in class. Some students do not participate in class because they are afraid or too nervous to do so. Since most discussions are over the textbook, students can anticipate what one or two of the questions are likely to be and practice answering them aloud. In fact, all students can improve their discussion skills by practicing the answers aloud to some of their SQ3R questions or end-of-the-chapter questions. Preparation for class discussions means having all the assignments done before class. It also means thinking of questions that will expand the discussion.

Become a Good Listener

You hear with your ears, but do you know how to listen? Listen and learn. Almost everything that you find on tests has been mentioned in class discussions and your teachers' lectures. If you listen carefully and jot down notes on what your teachers say, learning is much easier. It is important to learn how to listen in the classroom now, for in college many of your classes will be lectures.

Answer the following questions to determine if you know how to listen and learn in the classroom:

	Always	Sometimes	Never
1. Do I think about what I am hearing during class?	____	____	____
2. Do I stop listening when something is said that I find upsetting?	____	____	____
3. Do I listen for important points?	____	____	____
4. Do I listen for clues that suggest a major point is about to be made?	____	____	____
5. Do I let my mind drift instead of listening?	____	____	____
6. Am I easily distracted by other students?	____	____	____

Work on improving your listening skills by making goals for all your "never" answers.

Today's date _____

Listening skills goal # one _____

_____

_____

_____

Date in four weeks _____

Improvement noted _____

_____

_____

_____

_____

Today's date _____

Listening skills goal # two _____

_____

_____

_____

Date in four weeks _____

Improvement noted _____

_____

_____

_____

_____

Becoming a better listener

Distractions do affect your listening. The further back you sit, the more distractions there will be competing with the speaker. In addition, it is easy to be distracted, because the average person speaks at a rate of approximately 125 words a minute. Yet your listening power is much greater. That is why you have to make sure your mind is on track and not racing ahead or wandering miles off course in the wrong direction while the speaker just seems to be rambling along. Increase your attention by taking the following steps to become an active listener:

- Take notes over what is being said.
- Write questions to be asked later.
- Look for the speaker's most important ideas.
- Relate what you are hearing to information that you already have.
- Think about what the speaker is saying.

Use clues. Look at the following list of phrases that teachers use to indicate that what they are going to say next is important. Then add clues that several of your teachers use to this list. Get in the habit of waking up and listening when you hear these clues.

Listen carefully to this point.

I want to emphasize . . .

You should know the reasons . . .

The major cause was . . .

_____   _____

_____   _____

Take Class Notes

Taking good class notes is important in high school, but it is absolutely essential in college. In high school these notes help you remember what was discussed in class, give you useful explanations, let you recall the important things your teacher said, and supplement the material in your textbook. In college, these notes may be the major source of your information.

It is much easier to take notes on your textbook than it is to take notes in class. When you take textbook notes, you always have the opportunity to go back and reread the material. There are few second chances when you are taking notes in class. You must listen attentively. Then you have to choose what is important and organize those facts in your mind as you are writing them down in your own words.

Don't make the mistake of trying to copy down every word that your teacher is saying. You must learn to be selective and jot down only the important points. Be sure to write down all terms and definintions that are mentioned and anything that is ever written on the blackboard. You will find it helpful to take your notes in an outline form if your teachers present the material to you in an organized fashion.

Students who worry about having perfect notes are missing the boat. You should write them as neatly as you can because it is a waste of time to recopy them. During class just write your notes, then—as soon as possible after class—you should reread your notes to check for completeness and accuracy. After reviewing your notes, you may find it helpful to write a summary of them or to underline the important points.

Remember, lecture notes are not a substitute for reading your textbook. When lecturing, teachers usually give only a condensed version of what you will read in the textbook. One advantage of having lecture notes is that teachers often explain difficult textbook material during their lectures.

*Forging a Partnership
with Your Teachers*

Teachers have the job of teaching, but learning is your job. Both jobs are much easier if you are working together. Your attitude plays a big role in the success of this partnership. Teachers know the students who don't care enough to arrive in class on time. They also notice students who start packing up early. They see the students who yawn and take catnaps. Teachers are also aware of students doing other assignments, writing notes, and whispering with their friends. Some teachers will correct you, others will not. But all know that your behavior shows your attitude toward learning. They know whether you consider the classroom a social scene or a learning experience.

Talk to your teachers

You will not always understand everything that is being taught in your classes. However, you need to stay on top of the situation and get help quickly when you don't understand something, as most problems get larger—not smaller. Seek help from your teachers. They want you to succeed and can often help you turn things around in one brief meeting. Don't just talk to your teachers about academic problems, talk to them about what interests you in their classes.

How do your teachers see you?

One step involved in applying to many colleges is getting recommendations from your teachers. Often they are asked to fill out checklists comparing a student to other college-bound students. Fill out this checklist as you think your teachers would. It will give you a good idea of your strengths and weaknesses.

	Below Average	Average	Good	Excellent	Outstanding
Academic motivation					
Intellectual curiosity					
Personal initiative					
Academic self-discipline					
Creativity					
Energy					
Self-confidence					
Concern for others					
Sense of humor					
Emotional maturity					
Reaction to setbacks					
Respect accorded by teachers					
Respect accorded by peers					

Improving Your Reading

4

Consider how much reading you have done so far today, and you are still reading right now. It is almost impossible to do any schoolwork without reading. You may think that your high school work requires a lot of reading, but it is just a fraction of what you will do in college. In majors like history, English, economics, psychology, and political science all of your classes will require vast amounts of reading. In fact, only a few majors in college do not require considerable reading. Obviously, the more skilled you are at reading, the easier it is for you to acquire knowledge in high school and college. In this chapter, you will learn about ways in which you can improve your reading skills and the importance of setting up a reading program to prepare yourself for college admissions tests and courses.

How Much Do You Know about Reading?

Have you ever wondered exactly how much you know about reading? Test yourself right now by deciding whether the following statements are true or false.

1. It is impossible to improve your reading rate.   true   false

2. An average reader reads more than 400 words per minute.   true   false

3. Word-by-word reading does not affect your reading comprehension.   true   false

4. Your eye movements have nothing to do with your reading speed.   true   false

5. Skimming and scanning are the same skill.   true   false

6. Your vocabulary is not related to your reading comprehension.   true   false

7. As long as you know the main idea, you don't need to worry about the details.   true   false

8. Conclusions are always drawn for you in all your reading material.   true   false

9. The faster you read, the lower your comprehension will be.   true   false

10. The faster you read, the less you appreciate what you have read.   true   false

If you are knowledgeable about reading, you know that every statement above is false. Continue reading to learn how to improve your reading skills.

Banishing Bad Reading Habits

If you understand what you have read in this book so far, you have basic reading skills that will allow you to survive in high school and college. However, you may have some bad habits that are keeping you from being a really good reader. Complete these statements to find out more about your reading habits.

	Always	Sometimes	Never	
I	_____	_____	_____	read out loud to myself as I read.
I	_____	_____	_____	read at the same speed on all materials.
I	_____	_____	_____	backtrack over the material I have just read.
I	_____	_____	_____	use my finger or a pencil to point as I read.
I	_____	_____	_____	read one word at a time.
I	_____	_____	_____	have difficulty recognizing unfamiliar words.

Any statements that you completed with "always" or "sometimes" indicate bad reading habits. Continue reading to find out more about these bad habits and how to eliminate them before setting some new goals to improve your reading.

Reading out loud. Check that you are not also reading out loud when you read silently. Put your fingers over your lips right now as you are reading to see if you are moving them. Then put your fingers on your throat to see if you can feel any movement there. If you feel any movement in either place, it is a sign that you are saying words to yourself as you read. This habit slows down your reading because you can read much faster than you speak, and you are speaking.

To correct any lip movement, try holding a pencil tightly between your lips as you read. If you have movement in your throat, you should try chewing gum, eating, or sucking on something while reading.

Adjusting your reading speed. You need more than one reading speed. You should race through light reading and slow down on new textbook material that you are trying to learn. Consider your purpose when reading and then adjust your speed. Practice adjusting your speed by reading materials that require different speeds like a dictionary, a textbook, and newspaper comic strips.

Backtracking. Some students can scarcely read a line without going back once or twice to read a word again. You can stop backtracking by forcing your eyes to keep moving along a line. Use a card to cover what you have just read so it is impossible for you to backtrack.

Pointing. If you use any object to point as you read, it definitely slows your reading speed down. You can break this habit by placing a plain card or ruler under what you are reading.

Reading one word at a time. You read too slowly and don't make much sense out of what you are reading unless you read groups of words. To stop reading one word at a time, you will need to force yourself to read groups of words. You can make yourself flash cards with simple phrases on them, and you can read out loud with a good reader, trying to copy the good reader's phrasing.

Not recognizing unfamiliar words. If too many words are unfamiliar when you are reading, you need to increase your vocabulary. Before reading textbook materials, study the word lists. Then look unfamiliar words up in the glossary so you know you how to pronounce them and what they mean. Be sure to say the words so you will become accustomed to using them. You will find many additional vocabulary-building secrets in the next chapter.

Start to improve your reading skills by setting goals to eliminate your bad reading habits. You should notice improvement right away. Keep track of your progress on the following chart:

Today's date _____

Reading goal # one _____

_____

_____

_____

Date in four weeks _____

Improvement noted _____

_____

_____

_____

_____

Today's date _____

Reading goal # two _____

_____

_____

_____

Date in four weeks _____

Improvement noted _____

_____

_____

_____

_____

If you are not satisfied with your progress, you may need to take a reading course in high school. Such a course can make your high school and college work much easier.

Speeding Up Your Reading

Do you ever run out of study time and still have more reading assignments to finish? Perhaps you are reading too slowly. Do you think that you are reading as fast as you can? If you answered yes, you are probably wrong, because almost anyone can read faster. Eliminating bad reading habits is a first step in increasing your reading speed. The second step is simply to practice reading faster for short periods of time.

Find out exactly what your reading rate is now by timing yourself as you read the following 900-word-passage on franchising and fast foods. Before you start reading, make sure that you are in a comfortable place, preferably your own study area, and that you have eliminated all distractions. When you finish, you will be given the formula for calculating your reading rate. Begin by writing down the starting time in minutes and seconds or use a stopwatch.

Starting Time: _____

Franchising and Fast Foods

You may have heard the word *franchising* before, but do you really know what the word means? Franchising is a method of distributing products or services. It is the method used by fast food chains like McDonald's, Kentucky Fried Chicken, Mister Donut, and Burger King to increase their growth. However, not only established fast food companies use franchising as a way to grow, franchising also helps new fast food companies like D'Lites, Capt. Crab, and Zackly's make it in today's highly competitive fast food industry.

In franchising, there are two groups involved. The International Franchise Association describes them as the franchisor, who lends a trademark, a trade name, and a business system, and the franchisee, who wants to open the new unit. The franchisee will pay a royalty and often an initial fee for the right to do business under the franchisor's name and system. According to the association, the contract binding the franchisor and the franchisee is technically the franchise, but that term is often used to mean the actual business that the franchisee buys from the franchisor.

Fast food units can either be owned by the franchisor or the franchisee, and you usually cannot tell which one just by walking in the door of a restaurant. Whether you eat at a Wendy's, McDonald's, or Burger King that is owned by the company or a franchisee, the products, services, and quality should be the same.

When you buy a franchise, you are buying the name, the company's proven system for success, and its support not only in getting your unit open but also in handling any difficulties that you may encounter in doing business. The franchisor gives one-on-one help in such areas as advertising, purchasing, inventory control, and personnel management. However, don't think that successful franchising is automatic or easy. Franchising takes a lot of planning and skill along with considerable financial risk.

Many fast food franchisors will also assist the franchisee in obtaining a credit line, negotiating a lease, and receiving consent from zoning and planning boards. The fast food franchisor also provides the franchisee with operations manuals. In addition, the franchisor usually runs a training school that the franchisee is required to attend. The fast food franchisor also provides the franchisee with a manual that contains a record of the initial training procedures for all phases of management and recipes to be updated as methods change.

Burger King requires its franchisees to attend a training center for seven weeks where they learn cooking, personnel supervision, and selection and bookkeeping. Mister Donut holds a four-week training course for all new franchisees. A representative of the franchisee designated by the company is required to complete the training course to the company's satisfaction before the opening of the franchisee's Mister Donut shop and must also attend and complete any additional training and/or refresher courses prescribed by the company.

Franchisees must conduct their new businesses according to stipulations outlined by the franchisors in contracts. These stipulations encompass a broad range of franchise activities including such things as the precise amount of meat and spices to be put in a hamburger, the correct amount of time needed to cook a hamburger, and menu items that must be sold. The contract also deals with other matters like the hours of operation, inventory, insurance, personnel, and accounting. By establishing these stipulations in the contract, a franchisor is able to control costs and more importantly promote a unified brand image of identical outlets throughout a wide area.

When the franchise agreement is signed, both the franchisor and the franchisee have entered into a long-term relationship of perhaps as long as 20 years which may include an option to renew and extend the agreement. During that time, the franchisor will send district managers and inspectors regularly to visit the operating unit. This field service will provide advice and assistance to the franchisee on daily operations, check on the quality of the product and service, monitor the performance of the enterprise, and enforce regulations if necessary.

First of all, you can't just buy a franchise. There is a waiting list to become a franchisee at some of the chains. In fact, some people wait for several years. Then there is the matter of money. What fast food franchises cost varies enormously. You can expect to need start-up capital from approximately $40,000 to more than $400,000, and these figures do not include the land, the building, or improving the site, which could cost from over $100,000 to as much as $1 million. You should also know that some franchisors may require their franchisees to have a financial worth of at least $250,000 and ready cash of $200,000 or more. Although it may sound like it is impossible, it still is possible to buy a franchise. Start-up costs can be reduced substantially by leasing the land and/or building. In addition, some fast food chains help their long-time employees obtain their own franchises by providing them with low-interest loans and often leasing the building. An employee getting a franchise this way may only need as little as $50,000, which can be spent on start-up costs.

Although becoming a franchisee may appeal to you, you must also consider the disadvantages. The firm imposes strict controls. Quality of the product is regulated, and a large capital investment is required.

Stopping Time: _____

Determining how fast you read

Now to find out exactly what your reading rate was, you need to subtract your starting time from your stopping time or use your stopwatch time to get your total reading time: _____. Next, change your total reading time into seconds: _____. Then divide the 900 words in the passage by your total reading time in seconds to get your reading rate per second: _____. The last step is to multiply your reading rate in seconds by 60 to get your reading rate in words per minute: _____.

Most high school students should read a passage like the one you just read at a rate of between 200 to 300 words per minute. Your speed should drop down below 150 words per minute on very technical material. Then when you are reading for relaxation, your speed should accelerate. Reading experts believe that 800 words a minute is about as fast as anyone can really read material.

Practice to improve your reading speed

With practice, you can improve your speed, but you must be careful not to sacrifice understanding to get speed. Practice on a variety of materials. Read just two pages a day as fast as you can for a week, and you will begin to notice some improvement. Keep practicing, and your rate will keep improving. Remember to adjust your speed to suit the material. Keep track of your improvement on this chart.

My Reading Speed Chart
(words per minute)

Date	Pleasure reading	Textbook reading
_____	_____	_____
_____	_____	_____
_____	_____	_____
_____	_____	_____
_____	_____	_____

Move your eyes more efficiently

Try watching people's eyes as they read. Their eyes don't just glide smoothly across a page—they pause and then move on. When their eyes pause, they are reading. That pause is called a fixation, and if you can decrease the number of fixations that your eyes make, you will increase your speed.

The number of fixations that people make in reading a line is related to how much they see at each pause. So to reduce fixations, it is necessary to increase how much is seen in each pause. One way to practice doing this is to run your finger down the middle of a page and see how much you can see on either side of it. You can do the same thing by drawing a line down the center of a reading passage.

Skim and Scan Material

It seems like students have more to read every year they spend in school. So you have to be smart and know when you need to read every word and when it is sufficient to just read a few words here and there in a passage. After all, you don't read the entire telephone book when you look up a friend's phone number. In the same way, you shouldn't read the entire Constitution when you only need to know what the Twenty-fifth Amendment is. Skimming and scanning are the two skills that you use when it is not necessary or desirable to carefully read every word in a passage. While these skills are extremely helpful in high school, they are absolutely essential in college.

Skimming gives you the picture

Survey is the first step in the SQ3R method. When you survey a textbook, you are skimming. You are just reading enough to get the general idea of what the material is all about. In many cases, that means just reading the headings. You should do considerable skimming when you are doing research for reports and term papers. This means quickly glancing through an encyclopedia article on Herbert Hoover or automobiles to sense what information is given or thumbing through a book to see what topics are covered.

To skim, you read only headings, words in bold face or italic type, topic sentences, and paragraphs that grab your interest. Remember, you are not looking for anything specific. You are only trying to get an overview.

Scanning helps you find specifics

In scanning, like in skimming, your eyes must move quickly over the printed page. However, when you scan you know specifically what you are looking for, so your eyes must ignore most of the words as you search for a key word or phrase. You use scanning to find words like *Stamp Act, stamen,* and *ion* in your textbooks. Be sure to scan the next time you are trying to find a name or date in your social studies textbook.

Understanding What You Read

It is essential to be able to read fast enough to get through all your assignments each day. However, if you don't remember or understand what you read, your speed is not important. Testing your comprehension is not quite as easy as finding out your reading speed because there are five different skills that you must have to truly understand what you read.

Read the following passage, then answer the questions that follow. Each question tests a different comprehension skill.

History of Fast Food

The history of fast food restaurants from the first restaurant to the thousands that exist today is quite short because the fast food concept is so new. However, it did not take long for these restaurants to become a dynamic part of the food service industry.

People are intrigued with the speed and assembly-line efficiency by which meals are prepared in these restaurants, and this has kept them coming back. They like the way the fast food industry has always tried to serve food to its customers quickly, efficiently, and economically. A lot may have changed since the first fast food restaurants were started, but this has never changed.

The first settlers in America wanted quick, inexpensive meals, but there were few places to get them. Taverns were about the only spots where people could go to get a quick bite to eat, and free food was even served occasionally to those who purchased drinks.

Then came a great new invention that offered fast food service—the lunch wagon. These horse-drawn wagons sold sandwiches, slices of pie, and drinks round the clock in front of factories, parks, theaters, and other places where large crowds of people gathered. These wagons became larger and larger, and soon they were big enough for customers to step inside out of the wind and rain to order their food. In fact, some of these wagons even had places for customers to sit. It was not long until these wagons stopped traveling and parked in one spot.

After the Civil War, drugstores changed. It started when they began serving a new drink made out of sweet syrup and soda water. This drink became even more popular when someone thought of adding ice cream to it. Ice cream sodas became so well liked that most drugstores soon had soda fountains to serve them. Before long, soda fountains started adding different fast food items to their menus.

By the 1920s, many soda fountains had turned into luncheonettes. Coffee shops also started in the 1920s. People then had all these different places that served food faster than traditional restaurants. They could grab a sandwich as they passed a lunch wagon or sit on a stool and be served quickly at a soda fountain, luncheonette, or coffee shop. But even these restaurants did not satisfy the people's demand for fast food service, so cafeterias and other restaurants where people were willing to serve themselves emerged. These restaurants could feed a large number of people quickly.

Main Idea

1. What is this passage about?

_____

_____

_____

_____

_____

Details

2. What changed drugstores after the Civil War?

_____

_____

_____

_____

_____

Sequence

3. Were taverns or drugstores the first places to serve food quickly?

_____

_____

_____

_____

_____

Drawing Conclusions

4. Why has the fast food industry continued to grow?

_____

_____

_____

_____

_____

_____

Vocabulary

5. What does the word *efficiency* mean?

_____

_____

_____

_____

_____

You will find the answers to these questions as you read more about the different comprehension skills. In high school it is often most important to remember details for tests, but in college, besides knowing details, you have to know the main idea and be able to draw conclusions. Knowing vocabulary is always essential to comprehension while being able to sequence helps you organize information in your mind. When you take college entrance tests, you will have questions like the ones above that require you to use all the comprehension skills.

Finding the main idea   The passage you read was about the emergence of different kinds of fast food restaurants. In informational material, like this passage, authors use headings, introductory statements, and summaries to point out the main idea. Both the title and the introductory paragraph told you what the main idea of this passage on the history of fast food was.

In textbooks, each paragraph will have a main idea which is usually stated in a topic sentence. The topic is frequently the first sentence; however, it can be anywhere in the paragraph. Some paragraphs don't have topic sentences. In that case, you have to generalize what the main idea is from reading the entire paragraph. Once you train yourself to pick out the topic sentence or main idea of a paragraph, your comprehension will improve as you are selecting the most important idea from a mass of details. Write down the main idea of this paragraph.

Main idea _____

_____

_____

_____

_____

The main idea was stated in the first sentence, which was the topic sentence of the paragraph. Read the paragraph below on recalling details and try to pick out the topic sentence.

Topic sentence _____

_____

_____

Recalling details   Main ideas are important when you are studying, but to really learn a subject you need to remember details. For example, it is helpful to know the main idea of the passage on the history of fast food, but you won't really know much about that topic unless you know details about the taverns, lunch wagons, drugstores, and other places where food was served quickly. The answer to the question you were asked required knowing more details about drugstores. The answer was that drugstores started serving a new drink.

You will find it helpful to remember details in relation to the main idea rather than in isolation. Read the next paragraph for details, then note how they relate to the main idea.

There are job openings in the fast food industry at all levels. Everyone has heard about the shortage of workers for entry-level positions. There is also an excellent opportunity for people to become restaurant managers. If you choose to have a career in fast food, your chances for advancement are excellent. All this makes for a rosy job picture.

Main idea _____

_____

_____

_____

_____

_____

Related details _____

_____

_____

_____

_____

_____

Following sequence   You won't really understand the passage on the history of fast food unless you know the order in which different kinds of fast food places emerged. You should know that taverns served fast food before drugstores. Sequencing is an important part of reading comprehension. You need to know the order or sequence of events in history, obviously. But you also need to know the sequence of events in novels for your English class and experiments in your science class.

You can improve your sequencing skills by getting in the habit of writing down or retelling events in the order in which they occurred. Note how easy it would be to remember the order of the emergence of fast food places by completing this list.

1. taverns   4. luncheonettes

2. _____   5. _____

3. _____   6. cafeterias

Drawing conclusions   As you study, you have probably noticed that textbook authors usually sum up each chapter. They draw conclusions for you. However, you do read other materials like the "History of Fast Food" where you need to come to your own conclusions. You were asked why the fast food industry has continued to grow. After thinking about the information you were given, you should be able to put it together and come to the conclusion that the industry continues to grow because people want food that can be served fast.

Vocabulary

If you cannot understand key words when you are reading, it is difficult to truly understand what you are reading. Many times a word is defined in the text or you can guess what it means because it is related to a word you know. You were asked to define *efficiency*. This isn't too difficult because it is related to *efficient*, so you can determine that it means the quality of being efficient. And *efficient* means producing a result without causing any waste. The best way to increase your vocabulary is by doing a lot of reading. In the next chapter, you will read about more ways to improve your vocabulary.

Working on your comprehension skills

You must understand what you read. If you can't answer "yes" to all of the following questions, you need to set goals to improve your comprehension skills.

1. Can you recognize topic sentences?

2. Do you usually understand the main idea of a reading passage?

3. Are you able to recall details easily?

4. Can you retell the sequence of a series of events that you have read about?

5. Do you usually draw the correct conclusions from reading a passage?

6. Do you recognize most of the words in your reading assignments?

7. Do you usually understand what you read?

Today's date _____

Comprehension goal # one _____

_____

_____

_____

_____

Date in four weeks _____

Improvement noted _____

_____

_____

_____

_____

Today's date _____

Comprehension goal # two _____

_____

_____

_____

_____

Date in four weeks _____

Improvement noted _____

_____

_____

_____

_____

Read, Read, Read   One of the best ways to prepare for college is by reading—not just your school assignments or for relaxation but classic literary works. If you know what college you are planning to attend, write and ask the English department for a suggested reading list. You can also obtain good lists designed to help you prepare for college from your high school English teachers or the school librarian. Remember that new books are always coming on the market, so you will want to update any list that is more than three years old.

If you want to get started right now, you can use the following list that has been compiled from the lists of several colleges. First, read through the list and check off the books you have read. Then talk with friends, your parents, and teachers about which books on the list would be the best ones for you to read first. Circle these books and always use these books for book reports. The next step is to establish a reading program. Set aside 15 to 30 minutes each day for reading and enter that time on your personal study schedule. Such a program will be very effective in improving your reading skills, increasing your vocabulary, broadening your general knowledge, and preparing you for college admissions tests.

Aesop	fables
Agee, James	*A Death in the Family*
Alcott, Louisa May	*Little Women*
Anderson, Sherwood	*Winesburg, Ohio*
Auden, W. H.	poetry
Austen, Jane	*Pride and Prejudice*
Baldwin, James	*Go Tell It on the Mountain*
	The Bible
Bronte, Emily	*Wuthering Heights*
Browning, Elizabeth B.	poetry
Browning, Robert	poetry
Bunyan, John	*Pilgrim's Progress*
Camus, Albert	*The Fall*
	The Stranger
Carroll, Lewis	*Alice in Wonderland*
Cather, Willa	*Death Comes for the Archbishop*
Chaucer, Geoffrey	*The Canterbury Tales*

Chekhov, Anton	*The Cherry Orchard*
Conrad, Joseph	*Lord Jim*
Crane, Stephen	*The Red Badge of Courage*
Defoe, Daniel	*The Life and Strange Surprising Adventures of Robinson Crusoe, of York, Mariner*
Dickens, Charles	*A Tale of Two Cities*
	David Copperfield
	Oliver Twist
	Great Expectations
Doyle, Sir Arthur Conan	*Adventures of Sherlock Holmes*
Dreiser, Theodore	*An American Tragedy*
Ellison, Ralph	*Invisible Man*
Emerson, Ralph Waldo	essays
Faulkner, William	*Light in August*
Fermi, Enrico	*Atoms in the Family*
Fielding, Henry	*Shamela*
	Tom Jones
Fitzgerald, F. Scott	*The Great Gatsby*
Forster, E. M.	*A Passage to India*
Frank, Anne	*Diary of a Young Girl*
Franklin, Benjamin	*Autobiography*
Frost, Robert	poetry
Greene, Graham	*The Power and the Glory*
Hamilton, Edith	*Mythology*
Hawthorne, Nathaniel	*House of the Seven Gables*
	The Scarlet Letter
Heller, Joseph	*Catch-22*
Hemingway, Ernest	*For Whom the Bell Tolls*
Homer	*The Odyssey*
	The Iliad
Hugo, Victor	*The Hunchback of Notre Dame*
Ibsen, Henrik	*A Doll's House*
James, Henry	*The American*
	The Turn of the Screw

Kafka, Franz	*The Trial*
Kipling, Rudyard	*The Jungle Books*
Lawrence, D. H.	*Sons and Lovers*
	Women in Love
Lee, Harper	*To Kill a Mockingbird*
Lewis, Sinclair	*Babbitt*
	Main Street
London, Jack	*The Call of the Wild*
Mailer, Norman	*The Naked and the Dead*
Mann, Thomas	*The Magic Mountain*
Marquand, John P.	*Point of No Return*
Melville, Herman	*Moby Dick*
Mitchell, Margaret	*Gone with the Wind*
O'Neill, Eugene	*The Emperor Jones*
Orwell, George	*Animal Farm*
	1984
Ovid	*Metamorphoses*
Parkman, Francis	*The Oregon Trail*
Pasternak, Boris	*Dr. Zhivago*
Paton, Alan	*Cry, the Beloved Country*
Poe, Edgar Allan	tales and poems
Porter, William Sydney (O. Henry)	tales
Remarque, Erich	*All Quiet on the Western Front*
Roberts, Kenneth	*Robin Hood Tales*
Rolvaag, Ole Edvart	*Giants in the Earth*
Salinger, J. D.	*The Catcher in the Rye*
Sandburg, Carl	*Abraham Lincoln*
	poetry
Scott, Sir Walter	*Ivanhoe*
Shakespeare, William	*Hamlet*
	Henry IV
	Julius Caesar
	Macbeth
	Romeo and Juliet
Shaw, George Bernard	*Pygmalion*

Shelley, Mary	*Frankenstein*
Sophocles	*Oedipus Rex*
Steinbeck, John	*Of Mice and Men*
	The Grapes of Wrath
Stevenson, Robert Louis	*Treasure Island*
Stowe, Harriet Beecher	*Uncle Tom's Cabin*
Swift, Jonathan	*Gulliver's Travels*
Thackeray, William Makepeace	*Vanity Fair*
Thurber, James	*The Thurber Carnival*
Tolkien, J. R. R.	*Lord of the Rings*
Tolstoy, Leo	*War and Peace*
Twain, Mark	*The Adventures of Huckleberry Finn*
	The Adventures of Tom Sawyer
	Life on the Mississippi
Verne, Jules	*Around the World in 80 Days*
Wells, H. G.	*The Time Machine*
Wharton, Edith	*The Age of Innocence*
	Ethan Frome
Wilder, Thornton	*Our Town*
Williams, Tennessee	*A Streetcar Named Desire*
Woolf, Virginia	*To the Lighthouse*
Wright, Richard	*Black Boy*
	Native Son
Wyss, Johann David	*The Swiss Family Robinson*

Improving Your Basic Skills

Do you remember when you first rode a bicycle without training wheels? Think about that first ride. Then think about how you ride today. Many students don't seem to realize that their schoolwork, just like their bicycle riding, will improve if they spend enough time practicing on the basic skills needed for school.

If you work on your vocabulary, speaking, research, writing, and spelling skills, you will see improvement in your grades, find it easier to learn, and be preparing yourself for college. Without a solid background in these basic skills, it will be very difficult for you to handle higher skills, like critical reading and analyzing, that are required in college. You might even find it necessary to take remedial courses to learn these skills while you are in college. In this chapter, you will learn what you need to do to start improving your vocabulary, speaking, research, writing, and spelling skills.

Building Your Vocabulary

You will always learn a few new words every year without any effort. But that kind of vocabulary growth is not sufficient to build the vocabulary you need for high school, college, and college admissions tests. At this point in your education, you have to make an active effort to learn new words. As you increase your vocabulary, you will also be improving your reading rate and comprehension.

Learning vocabulary for admissions tests

Begin working on your vocabulary now so you won't be disappointed when you see your scores on the verbal sections of college admissions tests. How many of the following words which have appeared on these tests do you know?

1. sophisticated
2. indigenous
3. clique
4. paean
5. meticulous

6. complacent
7. gullible
8. truculent
9. embroil
10. olfactory

Did you know all of these words? Were you interested enough to look up any of the ones you didn't know? You need to have an interest in words if you truly want to build your vocabulary. Use one of the tools mentioned in the next section to learn the words that you did not know.

Tools for building your vocabulary

There are familiar tools that will help you increase your vocabulary. It is now time to start using these tools.

Dictionary. Don't be a student who uses the dictionary only to look up the meanings of words and does not use information in an entry about the pronunciation, synonyms, antonyms, parts of speech, or etymology of a word. Become interested in the study of words, especially the history of words. Many English words come from other languages.

Thesaurus. Do you find yourself in the habit of using the same words over and over again? If so, you should be using a thesaurus, which is a book of synonyms, to expand your vocabulary. The thesaurus helps you replace overused words like *big* and *little* with more exciting words like *ex-*

tensive, sizable, bantam, and *petite.* Use your thesaurus to find substitutes for the following overused words.

good _____ _____ _____

poor _____ _____ _____

happy _____ _____ _____

get _____ _____ _____

Flash cards. Flash cards are the best tool that you can use to teach yourself new words. Just by making the flash card, you are imprinting the word on your brain. Write the word on one side of the card and the definition on the other side. Add a synonym and an antonym for the word, and you have a wealth of information on one card. Flash cards can be used with a study partner, or you can use them alone.

Learning meaning from context clues

You will never get through your reading assignments if you need to look up a lot of words. Do you know the meaning of the words *heinous, perpetrated, atrocities, assimilate,* and *precipitated?* Read the following paragraph. You will meet the words that have just been mentioned. See if you can get the meaning of each word from the words around it in the paragraph.

Many *heinous* crimes were *perpetrated* in Paris during the French Revolution. Greedy villains invaded the residences of the royal families looting and committing *atrocities* against these defenseless citizens. Many of these royal citizens tried to *assimilate* themselves into the general population in hopes of escaping the spontaneous trials which *precipitated* an early death.

Now write the definition of the words. Use your dictionary if you need help.

1. heinous _____

_____

_____

2. perpetrated _____

_____

_____

3. atrocities _____

_____

_____

4. assimilate _____

_____

_____

5. precipitated _____

_____

_____

Breaking down and multiplying words

Words come in parts—prefixes, roots, and suffixes. If you know the meaning of the parts, you will often be able to figure out the meaning of the whole word. Learning the meaning of word parts is an easy way to increase your vocabulary.

Prefixes. Prefixes are the word parts that are found at the beginning of words. They help you start unlocking the meaning of a word. For example, the prefix *re-*means again, so the word *reread* means to read again. What do you think the words *reformulate, readmit,* and *reclassify* mean? You should learn to recognize some of the more commonly used prefixes and memorize their definitions. Here is a list of prefixes that you should know:

trans-	cross
hypo-	under
pro-	forward
il-	not
co-	with
mono-	one
retro-	back
ex-	out
bi-	two
ad-	to

Suffixes. The word parts at the end of words are called suffixes. You probably know that the suffix *-less* means without. If you add -less to the word *sense,* you form the word senseless, which means without sense.

Look at the list of common suffixes and their meanings and learn to recognize and use them to help you define unfamiliar words.

-able	capable of being	-ly	in the manner of
-hood	state of	-or	person who
-ness	like	-en	make or become
-ful	full of	-logy	study of

Roots. A root is the basic part of a word. Prefixes and suffixes are added to roots. You can expand your vocabulary by memorizing frequently used roots that come from Latin and Greek. For example, *crat* comes from the Greek word for rule or power. Write down all the words that you know that have this root:

autocrat, _____

_____

Compound words. Remember back in elementary school when you had fun joining two words together to form a new word—like dog + house = doghouse. See if you can join some of these words together to form compound words:

ad	slaughter	worthy	ship
fore	man	seer	partisan
over	close	here	note

_____   _____

_____   _____

_____   _____

Multiple meanings. You can hear the telephone *ring,* or you can wear a *ring.* Words with completely different meanings can be spelled the same. This can be confusing if you don't use context clues to know which meaning is intended. Can you think of another meaning for each of the following words?

1. reservation—keeping something back

   reservation _____

2. Waterloo—scene of Napoleon's final defeat

   waterloo _____

3. fleet—a group of warships

   fleet _____

Synonyms. Synonyms are words that have the same or nearly the same meaning. They expand your vocabulary and make what you say more precise and more interesting. A house can also be a residence or a dwelling. An order from a teacher should be obeyed; however, a command might be obeyed faster. Match each word in column 1 to its synonym in column 2.

column 1	column 2
_____1. keen	a. appall
_____2. overcome	b. disparity
_____3. inequality	c. apex
_____4. pinnacle	d. sharp
_____5. dismay	e. conquer

Answers: 1.d, 2.e, 3.b, 4.c, 5.a

Antonyms. On the SAT, you will be tested on your knowledge of antonyms. These are words that are opposite in meaning, for example, remain and depart and succeed and fail. Can you match the following antonyms?

_____1. robust	a. doe
_____2. buck	b. masculine
_____3. obese	c. apex
_____4. feminine	d. skinny

_____5. nadir   e. frail

Answers: 1.e, 2.a, 3.d, 4.b, 5.c

The secret to building a good vocabulary

It certainly helps to know about prefixes, suffixes, roots, synonyms, and antonyms, but the real secret is to read. The more you read, the more new words you are going to meet and learn from context clues. Read everything you can get your hands on—not just your textbooks. You should read magazines, the sports page, and some of the books from the suggested reading list in chapter 4. If you don't read because you find reading too difficult, then you have to start reading material that is easier until you become a more skilled reader.

Becoming a Better Speaker

Every day in some class you are probably expected to answer questions or participate in a discussion. As a speaker, you have the job of sending a message to your listeners. First, you have to make sure that you are prepared and have a message to send. Second, you have to send the message in such a way that your listeners receive it. Answer the following questions to see how you are doing as a speaker.

1. Do you monopolize classroom discussions?   yes   no
2. Do you rarely speak in class?   yes   no
3. Do you always take the position that you are right?   yes   no
4. Are you always negative?   yes   no
5. Do you frequently contradict others?   yes   no
6. Do you interrupt when someone else is speaking?   yes   no
7. Do you frequently try to change the topic of a discussion?   yes   no
8. Do you give only one-word answers to questions?   yes   no
9. Do you look at the floor, wall, or your desk when speaking in class?   yes   no
10. Do you always mumble or speak too softly?   yes   no

To be the best possible speaker in your high school and college classes, you need to answer "no" to these questions. Being aware of your speaking faults is the first step to correcting them. Then you need to make goals to improve your speaking skills.

Today's date _____

Speaking goal # one _____

_____

_____

_____

_____

Date in four weeks _____

Improvement noted _____

_____

_____

_____

_____

Today's date _____

Speaking goal # two _____

_____

_____

_____

_____

Date in four weeks _____

Improvement noted _____

_____

_____

_____

_____

How to ask questions

Participation in classroom discussions does not just mean answering questions. It also means asking them. You need to be curious enough about what you are studying to want more information as well as your classmates' and teachers' opinions. Skillful questioners know what type of question to ask to get the answer they want. A general question like "What can I learn from reading this book?" will let the person answering give a very broad reply. If you want to get a more specific answer, you need to ask a limiting question like "What page has information about financial aid?" When you are trying to gather in-depth information about a certain subject, you need to ask probing questions such as "Why do you consider the person who wrote this book an expert on financial aid?"

You probably have a number of questions about the college admissions process. Try writing down questions now that will get you the answers you need. Then ask your counselor or college advisor for the answers.

General question: _____

_____

_____

_____

_____

Limiting questions: (1) _____

_____

_____

_____

_____

(2) _____

_____

_____

_____

_____

Probing questions: (1) _____

_____

_____

_____

_____

(2) _____

_____

_____

_____

_____

(3) _____

_____

_____

_____

_____

How to answer questions

To answer questions effectively, you have to know what you are talking about. You can't do this if you haven't done your assignments. You also have to know what was asked. This means you have to listen to a question in order to answer it. Before you begin to answer a question, make an instant outline in your mind in order to organize what you say. Keep in mind that once you start to talk, what you say can never be erased. To improve your ability to answer questions, practice answering end-of-the-chapter questions aloud before class. You may find it helpful to do this in front of a mirror, or use a tape recorder to see how smoothly you answer questions.

How to handle oral reports

The most common kind of speech, outside of a speech class, is the oral report. What you are being asked to do is simply to give the same information that you would give in a written report in another way. You will need to have an introduction, a body, and a conclusion to your speech. Your topic should be narrow enough so that you can handle it in the few minutes you have to give your report. Like a written report, an oral report needs to be based on an outline. You can put the outline on note cards and use it when you are giving your speech. It is always better to give your report from a few note cards rather than an entire written report. This eliminates the possibility of your reading to instead of speaking to the class. When preparing an oral report, remember to organize your time so that you will be able to practice it aloud several times.

Developing Your Research Skills

Do you know where to look for information on careers in public service or the basic rules of baseball? Most students find that research is the hardest part of writing any paper or preparing an oral report. Research involves knowing where and how to find information. This is one skill that you will use repeatedly in college.

The library is the place where most high school students need to start their research. Even the smallest high school library is a vast storehouse of information. At the information desk of the library, you can usually obtain a pamphlet describing what material is available in the library and where it is located. You will not just find books but also newspapers, magazines, reference books, government documents, films, videos, records, and much more. If your library does not have what you are looking for, it may be able to use a computer to tap into a data base to find the material for you.

How to research in a library

Some students do not have a specific topic for a report or paper but want to explore material in the library on several topics before choosing one. Once you have selected a topic, you may find it necessary to narrow the topic even further after doing some research. It is often a good idea to read an article in an encyclopedia to get an overview of a topic before beginning any research. Where you begin your research depends on the timeliness of the topic. Research on current issues should begin with magazines, newspapers, and the vertical file, while research on less current topics can begin with books. As you become a more expert researcher, you will begin to use government documents, yearbooks, almanacs, and the wide array of indexes that help you find specialized information.

How to find a book

Whether you are doing research in your high school library or a college library, you follow exactly the same steps in finding a book. You go to the card catalog where all the books in the library are listed by title, author, and subject. For years this information was stored on cards in drawers, but now it is frequently stored in computers. You may even be able to get a printout of all the information.

To use the card catalog successfully, you need to know that all the cards are arranged in alphabetical order and that abbreviations are alphabetized as if they were spelled out. Also, do not pay any attention to *a, an,* or *the* in titles when searching for a book.

The Dewey Decimal System. The number you will find on the card, as you probably know, is the call number, and it is also on the spine of the book to help you find it. If a library uses the Dewey Decimal System, books will be numbered according to these classifications:

Numbers	Major Divisions	Subdivisions
000-99	General Works	encyclopedias, bibliographies, periodicals
100-199	Philosophy	logic, psychology, religion
200-299	Religion	
300-399	Social Sciences	political science, economics, law, education, government

400-499	Language	dictionaries, grammars
500-599	Pure Science	mathematics, physics, astronomy, chemistry, biology
600-699	Technology	medicine, engineering, agriculture, business, radio, TV
700-799	The Arts	architecture, sculpture, painting, music, sports
800-899	Literature	novels, poetry, plays
900-999	History and Geography	

The Library of Congress System. Some large libraries use the Library of Congress Classification System (LC). The books in this system are classified using twenty-one letters of the alphabet to group books by major subject areas.

A. General Works	N. Fine Arts
B. Philosophy, Psychology, and Religion	P. Language and Literature
C, D, E, F. History	Q. Science
G. Geography, Anthropology, and Recreation	R. Medicine
H. Social Sciences	S. Agriculture
J. Political Science	T. Technology
K. Law	U. Military Science
L. Education	V. Naval Science
M. Music	W. Bibliography and Library Science

Browsing can be helpful. Once you have found a book on the library shelves, look at the other books next to it, as they are on related topics. You may find other books that you want to investigate further.

How to find a magazine article

When students used to look for articles on a subject in nontechnical magazines, they always consulted the *Reader's Guide,* which was in book form. Today, you can also find the same information on microfiche, microfilm, and computers. You will find both author and subject entries.

Specific subjects. Many students don't seem to know about the extraordinary number of magazines that are written on specific subjects. Information about these magazines will not be found in indexes like *Reader's Guide* but in specific subject indexes like the following ones:

Current Index to Journals in Education

Art Index

The Music Index

Biological and Agricultural Index

Business Periodical Index

Micro Computer Index

How to find more information

Information in a library is certainly not limited to books and magazines. The better you understand what other sources of information there are, the easier it will be for you to do research. Spend time browsing through the reference section in a library until you become thoroughly acquainted with the following materials. It will make your research much easier. Don't ever forget to get help from librarians—they truly know how to research every subject.

Encyclopedias. Most students use general encyclopedias, which have information on just about everything.

There are also specialized encyclopedias on subjects like the following ones:

baseball	historic forts
wildlife	shells
education	awards

Atlases. If you are looking for any type of map—physical, population, political—there are atlases that will provide this information.

Almanacs. When you want up-to-date facts and statistics about such things as sports, noted personalities, world events, astronomical events, or ZIP codes, you will find them in almanacs, which are published once a year.

Handbooks. These books give an overview of one or more subjects and are arranged for quick location of facts. The title of the handbook usually indicates what material will be covered, such as *The East European and Soviet Data Handbook.*

Yearbooks. Put out each year, yearbooks give you a summary of facts and statistics of the preceding year. They often are limited to one subject, like *Yearbook of the United Nations.*

Bibliographies. These reference books help you find books in various subject areas, like books on history or psychology. If you are unfamiliar with bibliographies, you should look at *Guide to Reference Books,* which will help you locate reference books.

Newspapers. Most libraries have local newspapers as well as access on microfilm or microfiche to major newspapers like *The New York Times* or *Wall Street Journal.*

How good is a source?
You may find it difficult to decide which sources to use. Ask yourself the following questions to decide which sources are the best ones:

1. How many pages are devoted to the subject you need?

2. What is the publication date? For example, if you are writing about current space flights you will not want a book that was written in the 1970s.

3. What are the author's qualifications?

4. Can I read the material?

5. Does the source offer special features like maps, charts, and illustrations?

Improving Your Writing Skills
Take courses that require you to write in high school, for in college your entire grade for a quarter or semester may depend on a paper or essays written on a final examination. When teachers return your written work, study the errors that you have made because these are the areas that require your attention. Now determine if you have mastered the skills essential to good writing.

1. Do you know how to make note cards?   yes   no

2. Can you write a bibliography?   yes   no

3. Do you choose narrow topics?   yes   no

4. Can you outline a paper?   yes   no

5. Do you know how to use good grammar?   yes   no

6. Can you write an introduction, body, and conclusion for a paper?   yes   no

If there are any areas in which you cannot confidently answer "yes," you need to set goals to improve those areas.

Today's date _____

Writing goal # one _____

_____

_____

_____

Date in four weeks _____

Improvement noted _____

_____

_____

_____

_____

Today's date _____

Writing goal # two _____

_____

_____

_____

_____

Date in four weeks _____

Improvement noted _____

_____

_____

_____

_____

The writing process   The moment students receive an assignment, they need to organize their time. Too many students devote too much time to research and too little time to writing and proof-reading. Before beginning to write, students need to make an outline. This is an easy task for a research paper when you have note cards. By simply sorting the cards into an appropriate order, you can create an outline.

When you write your first draft, you want to achieve a balance between writing so fast that your paper is full of errors and plodding so slowly that your paper loses all of its spontaneity. Proofreading is the vital process that makes every paper the best it can be. All students need to develop a list of questions that they will use as a guidepost for catching errors. Read the first two paragraphs of the rough draft of a high school student's paper. You will note numerous errors. Use the student's checklist to find those errors and then correct them.

Steroids in the Sports World

Drugs has become a major problem in sports. one of the most misabused drugs in the world of sports is steroids. Athletes turn to steroids for many reasons, but mostly because they don't want to let down their team and coach because steroids have just recently become a problem, the head committees of sports is not sure how to solve this problem. It is the thesis of this paper that all athletes should be tested for the use of steroids before a major athletic competition.

A big part of all sport competitions is the fairness issue. When using steroids they gain an advantage over their competitors because they vecome physically stronger. The American college of sports Medicine doesn't think that using steroids are fair. The collige strongly sees the need for equality in competition and the good health of the participants. They see nonsteroid use in the best interest of all sports. Dtr. Good a clinical psychologist who specializes in shemical dependency also believe that fairness plays a big part in sports and that taking short-cuts is not fair, especially when the athlete know the rules. The governing bodies set the rules and principlals regarding the use of drugs and expect them to be followed.

General questions

1.	Is the thesis clearly stated in the introduction?	yes	no
2.	Will the reader understand what is said?	yes	no
3.	Does the conclusion sum up the whole paper?	yes	no
4.	Is the information presented in logical order?	yes	no
5.	Does the vocabulary sound natural?	yes	no

Paragraphs

1.	Does each paragraph have a topic sentence?	yes	no
2.	Does each paragraph have at least three sentences?	yes	no
3.	Do the paragraphs flow together smoothly?	yes	no

Sentences

1. Does every sentence express a complete thought?   yes   no

2. Are there any run-on sentences?   yes   no

3. Do all sentences begin with a capital letter?   yes   no

4. Are all sentences correctly punctuated?   yes   no

5. Do all subjects and verbs agree in person and number?   yes   no

Words

1. Are all words spelled correctly?   yes   no

2. Are all pronoun antecedents clear?   yes   no

3. Are there any dangling or misplaced modifiers?   yes   no

4. Have the best words been selected?   yes   no

Working on Your Spelling Skills

Spelling words in the English language is difficult because so many frequently used words do not follow any of the rules. Check your own spelling right now. Circle the word in each row that is spelled correctly.

	Column A	Column B
1.	acadamy	academy
2.	acomodate	accommodate
3.	admissable	admissible
4.	accurate	acurate
5.	allegiance	allegience
6.	aquit	acquit
7.	beleive	believe
8.	bookkeeper	bookeeper
9.	calender	calendar
10.	confered	conferred
11.	conference	conferrence
12.	cushon	cushion
13.	definately	definitely
14.	deterant	deterrent
15.	divisable	divisible
16.	eficient	efficient
17.	ieght	eight
18.	hopeing	hoping
19.	kahki	khaki
20.	mischief	mischef

Answers: 1.B, 2.B, 3.B, 4.A, 5.A, 6.B, 7.B, 8.A, 9.B, 10.B, 11.A, 12.B, 13.B, 14.B, 15.B, 16.B, 17.B, 18.B, 19.B, 20.A

Spelling is seeing words

Did you know that people learn how to spell words by seeing them? Make sure you actually see words as well as hear them. Close your eyes and picture a word as you say the word aloud to yourself. Some words look alike and even sound alike which can be confusing. Match the word in column I to its look-alike word in column II.

	Column I	Column II
_____	1. extant	a. duel
_____	2. dual	b. whole
_____	3. flair	c. hopping
_____	4. hole	d. hare
_____	5. hoping	e. lone
_____	6. idle	f. male
_____	7. hair	g. knew
_____	8. loan	h. extent
_____	9. mail	i. lien
_____	10. new	j. aural
_____	11. lean	k. flare
_____	12. oral	l. idol

Answers: 1.h, 2.a, 3.k, 4.b, 5.c, 6.l, 7.d, 8.e, 9.f, 10.g, 11.i, 12.j

The problem of mispronouncing words

Do you ever mispronounce a word? The following words are often mispronounced, causing the speller to add an extra vowel. Take out the extra vowel in each word and write the word correctly.

	word	extra vowel	correct spelling
1.	disasterous	_____	_____
2.	enterance	_____	_____
3.	grievious	_____	_____
4.	hinderance	_____	_____
5.	hundered	_____	_____
6.	laundary	_____	_____
7.	monsterous	_____	_____

8. partener _____ _____

9. similiar _____ _____

10. umberella _____ _____

Reviewing common spelling rules

1. The *ei-ie* rule.

Write *i* before *e*, except after *c*, or when sounded like *a* as in n*ei*ghbor and w*ei*gh. There are some exceptions to this rule like protein and weird.

See if you really know how this rule works. Try spelling the following words correctly by using *ei* or *ie*.

1. __ght	6. f__ld
2. y__ld	7. c__ling
3. ach__ve	8. dec__ve
4. cash__r	9. v__l
5. r__gn	10. rec__pt

Answers: 1. eight 2. yield 3. achieve 4. cashier 5. reign 6. field 7. ceiling 8. deceive 9. veil 10. receipt.

2. The final *y* rule.

Words ending in *y* preceded by a consonant usually change *y* to *i* before any suffix except one beginning with *i.* Words ending in *y* preceded by a vowel do not change *y* to *i* before suffixes or other endings. You need to be careful when using this rule because there are a lot of exceptions to it. Following the final *y* rule, add the suffixes *-ed* and *-ing* to these words:

	add-ed		add-ing
try	_____	try	_____
stay	_____	stay	_____

Answers: tried, trying, stayed, staying

3. The final *e* rule.

If the final *e* in a word is silent, it is usually dropped before a suffix beginning with a vowel but is retained before a suffix beginning with a consonant. See how well you can handle the final *e* rule as you add endings to the following words. Rewrite each word.

	add ing		add less
argue	_____	care	_____
believe	_____	use	_____
judge	_____	hope	_____
like	_____	age	_____

Answers: arguing, believing, judging, liking, careless, useless, hopeless, ageless.

4. The plural of nouns ending in *o* rule.

Nouns ending in *o* preceded by a vowel add *s* to form the plural. Nouns ending in *o* preceded by a consonant add *es* to form the plural. Circle whether you would add *s* or *es* to form the plural of the following words. There are a few exceptions to this rule.

1. auto   s es   4. hero   s es

2. potato s es   5. radio s es

3. patio   s es   6. echo   s es

Answers: 1.s, 2.es, 3.s, 4.es, 5.s, 6.es.

How to learn to spell words Use the following five steps when you want to learn to spell new words.

1. Say the word while looking at it.
2. Close your eyes, try to see the word, and then spell the word aloud.
3. Check to see if the word was spelled correctly.
4. Cover the word and write it.
5. Check again to see if the word is spelled correctly.

If the word is misspelled, go back to step one and repeat all the steps again. If you can't spell all the words on the following list of commonly misspelled words, use the five steps to learn how to spell these words.

1. absence	14. haughtiness
2. accept	15. irritable
3. according	16. license
4. ache	17. narrative
5. across	18. peculiarities
6. beginning	19. personnel
7. careless	20. receipt
8. chocolate	21. seriousness
9. commission	22. specimen
10. despair	23. theories
11. divide	24. whether
12. enormous	25. zenith
13. fallacy	

Make a list of all words that you misspell on school papers. Then use the five steps to learn these words.

Becoming an Expert Test Taker

During your school years you will take a great number of tests. Some will be teacher-made while others are created by textbook publishers, and from time to time you will take standardized tests. Taking tests will not stop when you graduate from high school. There are plenty of tests waiting for you in college and even in your career. In this chapter, you will learn more about the different kinds of tests you take at school and how to study for each one. You will also learn why tests are given and how to become an expert at taking them.

Why Tests Are Given

Tests are not given to make your life miserable. There are solid reasons why they are given:

- Teachers need to find out what you have learned and what you still need to learn.

- Teachers need to evaluate their own teaching.

- By law, your achievement in different subjects often needs to be compared to that of other students in your state and the nation.

- Tests are given to determine who needs or is eligible for special programs.

- Tests are given to place students of similar abilities in the same groups.

- College admissions officers want a more complete picture of your aptitude for college.

- Employers want to know more about your skills before they hire you.

The Secrets of Preparing for Tests

Do you ever feel like you are hitting your head against a brick wall? Do you spend hours studying for a test, feel confident you are really prepared, then end up not doing well on the test? Being test-wise is a skill that some students master much faster than others. If you haven't mastered it yet, start now. You don't want to continue hitting your head against the test wall in college.

Ask yourself the following questions to determine if you prepare correctly for tests:

1. Do I use my class time to begin learning the material?   yes   no

2. Do I keep up with the class reading assignments and homework?   yes   no

3. Do I use SQ3R, outline, or take notes when I read my textbooks?   yes   no

4. Do I take notes in class?   yes   no

5. Do I follow a study schedule?   yes   no

6. Do I schedule frequent review sessions for each class?   yes   no

7. Do I make sure I know what topics will be covered on tests by listening for hints from the teacher before the test?   yes   no

8. Do I see if there are study copies of old tests to use in preparing for tests?   yes   no

9. Do I study what I don't know?   yes   no

10. Do I make it a point to learn all key words in a chapter for a test?   yes   no

11. Do I read all chapter summaries and answer all end-of-the-chapter questions in preparation for a test?   yes   no

12. Do I schedule sufficient study time for tests?   yes   no

Select two of the questions that you answered "no" and set yourself the goal of turning the answers to "yes" to begin improving your preparation for tests.

Today's date _____

Test preparation goal # one _____

_____

_____

_____

_____

Date in four weeks _____

Improvement noted _____

_____

_____

_____

_____

Today's date _____

Test preparation goal # two _____

_____

_____

_____

_____

Date in four weeks _____

Improvement noted _____

_____

_____

_____

_____

Knowing what a test will be like

Half of the secret of preparing for tests is knowing what a test will be like. If the teacher does not provide you with this information, you must ask the following questions. Copy these questions into your assignment notebook so that you will be prepared with your questions before the next test.

1. What will the test cover (class discussions, chapters or pages in textbook, other)?

2. What type of test will it be (objective or essay)?

3. What kinds of questions will there be (multiple choice, short answer, true-false, other)?

4. How much time will be allotted for the test (entire class period or minutes)?

5. How will the test be answered (blue book, on test copy, answer sheet)?

6. Are there penalties for guessing?

7. Does every question on the test have equal value?

8. How will the test be graded?

9. What special supplies will I need?

Knowing how to study for tests

The major mistake that most students make in studying for tests is trying to reread all the material. Instead, students need to concentrate on learning what teachers have told them will be on tests. They should underline those points in their class notes, book notes, outlines, SQ3R questions, study guides, and assignments. Then they should review only this underlined material, paying attention to what they don't know rather than spending time on what they already know. For all classes, it is almost always essential to know the words that are listed under headings like vocabulary, important terms, and word lists. Finally, how students need to study for a test depends on what kind of test they will be taking.

Different Kinds of Tests

If you have been observant during your school years, you will have noticed that sometimes your teachers give you tests that they have made, and other times they use tests made by textbook companies. Teacher-made tests usually test what teachers believe their students should have learned from both class discussion and the textbook. On the other hand, textbook companies do not know what has been emphasized in class, so their tests will be based on material in the textbook.

Most high school tests, no matter who made them, have an objective format, which means you are required to select or supply an answer. Less common are essay tests where students may have to write from a paragraph to several pages on a topic. In the next section, you will read about five different kinds of tests. Use a pencil or a highlighter to underline the important points that will help you improve your scores on these tests.

Multiple choice: a choice of answers

Multiple choice questions are made up of two parts. The incomplete statement or question is called the stem. It is followed by a list of possible answers called the options. The directions usually ask you to select the answer that is the best option. Problems occur when students hurry through the stem to get to the options. If you don't really understand what the stem is asking, reread it before looking at the options. Then read all the options before you select one. Remember, you are looking for the best answer—not just a good answer. Be careful, because several of the options will seem good. It is helpful to cross out options that are not good answers so you can concentrate on selecting the best answer from the remaining options. Every time you eliminate even one option you are increasing your chances of finding the right answer. It will also help if you remember these right-answer clues:

- Options that are very precisely stated are probably correct.

- Options that are noticeably longer than others often have added information to make the option correct.

Studying for multiple choice tests. Complete the following multiple choice test question.

Multiple choice tests require a knowledge of _____

a. details   c. principles

b. relationships   d. all of the above

Answer: (d) all of the above.

Matching tests measure factual knowledge

Matching tests usually have two columns of information. You have the job of matching each entry in one column to the correct response in the other column. Don't be surprised if occasionally you take a matching test that has more than two columns.

Read the directions for matching tests very carefully, as answer choices can sometimes be used more than once. It is usually easier and faster if you work from the column that has the most information and try to find the correct response in the column with less information. Make sure you cross out responses as you use them unless a response can be used more than once. When you can't match an item, go on and come back to it when you have completed the column. It will be easier to determine the correct answer from the remaining choices.

When studying for matching tests, remember that these tests are designed to measure your recall of factual information. Make sure you review specific facts like rules, formulas, dates, definitions, and names. Making flashcards for all the important facts is a good way to prepare for this type of test.

Complete this sample matching exercise by matching the test to what it measures.

Name of test	Measurement of
____1. achievement	a. aptitude for college work
____2. college admissions	b. physical aptitudes
____3. intelligence	c. knowledge in a skill area
	d. intellectual ability

Answers: 1.c, 2.a, 3.d.

True-false means two choices

True-false tests give you a choice of two answers with only one answer being the correct response. Preparation for these tests should be similar to that for multiple choice tests as they also test your knowledge of facts.

After reading a statement, decide if it is true or false. If you are unsure of the answer, remember your first response is often the correct one. You need to notice words like *usually, generally, sometimes,* and *often.* They are so broad that they are usually found in true statements. However, words like *always, all, never,* and *none* usually indicate a false statement. Always answer all true-false questions, as you have a 50 percent chance of being correct.

Take the following true-false test. Put a circle around either the T or F.

1. All tests can be prepared for in the same way. T F

2. Teachers sometimes use tests prepared by textbook companies. T F

3. It is never a good idea to question your teachers about what will be on a test. T F

4. You need to know what kind of a test you will be taking to know how to prepare for it. T F

Answers: 1.F, 2.T, 3.F, 4.T.

Completion tests: blanks to fill in

In this type of test you are required to supply the correct word, phrase, names, numbers, dates, or symbols to complete a statement. You will sometimes be given a word bank with the correct answers to help you out. You should prepare for this test in the same way as you would prepare for any test of specific factual knowledge while paying particular attention to vocabulary.

Use the word bank to fill in the answers on the completion test. These words are frequently used in the directions for essay tests.

word bank: analyze   discuss

explain   identify

1. Breaking something down into smaller parts to look at it closer is to _____.

2. To point out the personal distinguishing characteristics is to _____ something.

3. To consider and argue the pros and cons of something is to _____.

4. To make clear what something means is to _____ it.

Answers: 1. analyze, 2. identify, 3. discuss, 4. explain.

Essay tests require organization

This type of test often scares students. It shouldn't, because it is possible to figure out what is going to be on an essay test. Essay questions usually cover the main points that have been discussed in your class or textbook. You will also have to know the details that are related to these main points. Unlike most of the other tests mentioned in this section, an essay test requires you to recall the answer rather than to recognize it. Prepare for this type of test by writing out answers to questions that you have made up or questions at the end of a chapter. You will frequently find that you have answered actual essay questions by preparing in this way.

On essay tests, you will do better if you take a moment to organize your answers. Some students jot down a quick outline before they start writing longer essays. Strive to write clearly and to use good grammar. Make an effort to use the proper technical vocabulary, as it will let your teachers see that you not only have learned the terms but also are able to use them correctly. Remember, if you don't write something, you will not receive any credit for an answer. When you aren't sure of an answer, write down what you do know on the topic to get partial credit. Many times just starting to write an answer brings the answer to you. Don't forget to write your essays neatly so that teachers are able to read your work.

Answering An Essay Question

Try your hand at answering the following essay question: Discuss the difference between preparing for an essay test and an objective test like a multiple choice, matching, true-false, or completion test.

_____

_____

_____

_____

_____

_____

_____

_____

_____

_____

_____

Becoming an Expert at Taking Tests

Now check and see if you do all the right things when you are taking tests. Ask yourself the following questions:

1. Do I always arrive in the classroom early?   yes   no

2. Do I remember to bring all necessary supplies?   yes   no

3. Do I remain calm?   yes   no

4. Do I always look over the entire test before beginning it?   yes   no

5. Do I read the directions carefully before doing each section of a test?   yes   no

6. Do I budget my time?   yes   no

7. Do I answer the questions I know first?   yes   no

8. Do I check my answers if there is time?   yes   no

9. Do I believe in my ability to do well?   yes   no

Select two questions that you answered with a "no" and set goals so that you will see improvement in those areas.

Today's date _____

Test-taking goal # one _____

_____

_____

_____

Date in four weeks _____

Improvement noted _____

_____

_____

_____

Today's date _____

Test-taking goal # two _____

_____

_____

_____

Date in four weeks _____

Improvement noted _____

_____

_____

_____

After the test is over   Whether you receive an A or a C, there are still things to do when a corrected test is returned to you.

- Take the time to review it.

- Find out the answers to all missed questions and write them down.

- Note what kind of errors you are making so you can avoid them on future tests.

- Keep the test, if possible, so you can use it to review for semester exams.

School Is More Than Books

Colleges want students with sound academic records. But they also want students who have shown the energy to participate in extracurricular activities, hold jobs, volunteer for community activities, and travel. Furthermore, they want students to show excellence in these nonacademic activities as well as enthusiasm in pursuing them.

Although grades and test scores are usually the most important considerations for admission to college, extracurricular activities and work experience can play an important role, especially for selective schools. But more than that, these activities can contribute immensely to the personal development of students during their high school years. In this chapter, you will find out how you can get far more from high school than book learning by taking an energetic part in activities outside the classroom.

Extracurricular Activities: Part of Your High School Career

Extracurricular activities are a training ground for college and career. You learn how to interact with other people as you build floats for homecoming parades, run with the cross country team every morning before school, and play in the pep band. You pick up very real organizational skills by planning club meetings and the Junior Prom or by being the manager of a sport. What's more, you learn how to meet deadlines. Yearbooks and newspapers have to be put out on time, and minutes have to be ready for club meetings. There is also the opportunity to develop your leadership skills. You don't have to be the president of an organization to do this. You can take charge of a committee to clean up after an event or to make posters for a car wash. The more practice you have at doing these things, the more skilled an individual you will become. There is one added dividend that you gain by participating in extracurricular activities—they are a lot of fun.

Finding your activity

You find out about what activities your school has by reading the student handbook and listening to daily announcements over the P.A. that tell you what is going on at your school. Some schools even have open houses at the start of the school year where you can talk with representatives from each activity. With such a large choice of activities, how do you choose the ones in which you will participate? The answer is to use your interests as a guide. Check the activities on the following list that tie most closely with your interests. Add to the list, if appropriate.

_____	sports	_____	academic clubs
_____	student government	_____	service clubs
_____	publications	_____	hobby clubs
_____	band, orchestra	_____	TV and radio stations
_____	choir	_____	drama
_____	dance	_____	speech
_____	cheerleading	_____	debate
_____	_____	_____	_____

Making a commitment

Your first year in high school is the time to investigate several activities to see which ones really interest you. Then in the remaining years of high school you should try to concentrate on just a few activities rather than jumping from activity to activity. The student who joins the drama club and first works as a prompter and then has minor roles in several plays before actually directing a play has shown the ability to make a commitment and stick to it. This is an admirable quality that college admissions officers and future bosses regard as important. An ability to commit oneself to an activity for a considerable period of time indicates maturity. Make the goal now to commit yourself to excellence in one activity this year.

Today's date _____

Extracurricular activity goal _____

_____

_____

_____

_____

Date in four weeks _____

Improvement noted _____

_____

_____

_____

_____

Using your time wisely

Some activities require extraordinary amounts of time. Sports teams practice every day. School plays require daily rehearsals. Putting out the yearbook requires a year of almost daily work sessions. Most students can handle only one major extracurricular activity at a time and do justice to their schoolwork. If you can answer the following questions with a definite "yes," then you probably are handling the demands on your time from extracurricular activities well.

1. Do you complete all your homework every day?   yes   no

2. Do you have sufficient time to prepare for tests?   yes   no

3. Are you getting enough sleep?   yes   no

4. Are you receiving the best grades you can?   yes   no

5. Are you enjoying both your schoolwork and your extracurricular activities?   yes   no

"No" answers indicate problems. You may be overcommitted to an activity or trying to participate in too many activities. Even though extracurricular activities provide tremendous amounts of satisfaction, you always have to remember that your first priority must be doing well in school.

Volunteering Should Have a Place

So many people's lives are more pleasant because someone volunteered time to help an individual or an organization. High school students should try to use some of their energy on volunteer activities. Not only is volunteering very rewarding, it is setting a precedent for a lifetime of aiding those who need some special help. The list of volunteer activities is long. Why don't you consider volunteering?

_____ assistant scout leader	_____ tutor
_____ election campaign worker	_____ sports coach
_____ library assistant	_____ reader for the blind
_____ recycling worker	_____ aide to a politician
_____ nursing home aide	_____ hospital aide

A Steady Job Is a Learning Experience

Finding a steady job and keeping that job shows a maturity that college admissions officers like to see in candidates for admission to their schools. They also like to see students exercise initiative in their jobs that results in promotions or interesting job assignments. Students who participate seriously in extracurricular activities may not have the time to hold a part-time job during the school year, but they can work in the summer. Jobs offer a preview of the world of work. They teach students to arrive on time, work every day, get along with bosses who may be difficult, and stick with a task.

There are negatives to students holding jobs during the school year. Jobs can take time away from studying and encourage students to value working more than studying because they are earning money. Jobs can also prevent students from participating in extracurricular activities.

Traveling Adds to Students' Experiences

Whenever students have the opportunity to travel, they should do so whether it is on a family trip or as an exchange student. It is an easy way to learn geography, some history, and a lot about people in different parts of this country and the world. Being an exchange student is a particularly valuable experience as it offers an opportunity to learn about how people in other cultures live and may give students practice in speaking another language.

Activities Outside the Classroom Are Important

If you always watch more than an hour of television a day, talk on the telephone for endless hours, or just hang around with your friends most of the time, you are not using your time outside the classroom to your greatest advantage. You should be spending more time on extracurricular activities, volunteering, and working. These activities add something extra to your life. They teach you skills that can't be learned in the classroom.

HOW TO GET INTO COLLEGE

Section II

Organizing the College Admissions Process

There are over 3,000 colleges in the United States. Some are large schools with thousands of students while some may be smaller than your own high school. Colleges are located in tropical paradises, large cities, and your own hometown. You could be happy and do well at a great number of colleges. Deciding which colleges would be most suitable for you and then applying to them is not an easy task. It requires organization.

You have to make sure that you take the right courses in high school. There are tests that must be taken by certain dates. Colleges need to be visited. Application deadlines have to be met. In this chapter, you will find out how to organize the admissions process. This is not something that should be left until you are a senior in high school. There are too many things to be done to wait that long. Ideally, preparing for admission to college should begin during the ninth grade. You need to find out early which colleges offer what you want and where you can expect to be accepted.

Keeping a Record of Your High School Career

The very first step in organizing the college admissions process is to start keeping a record of what you have done during high school. You will use this information when you begin to fill out college applications. Save samples of your work like essays and art projects. You should also keep newspaper clippings that mention your accomplishments. It is smart to keep all official reports of grades in case the school makes an error on your transcript. Results of college admissions tests should also be kept. The best place to keep all these records is in a folder or large envelope. Put each year's record in a separate folder or envelope.

Important information to record

You need a written record of what you have done in high school. When you are filling out college applications, it is easy to forget that you were a volunteer scout leader during the summer of your freshman year when you were working at a fast food restaurant or that you won first place in an essay contest sponsored by a local service club when you were a sophomore. Remembering information like this could play a part in your being accepted at a college. You should keep the following information:

Grades. On many college applications, especially those for state schools, you will be asked to report what courses you have taken and the grades you have received. You will need to write down the specific name of each course. Colleges don't want to know that you studied English as a freshman in high school but, more specifically, whether it was a class in composition, American literature, or speech.

Test scores. Part of the admissions process for most colleges is the taking of the SAT, ACT, and Achievement Tests. Some schools will even want to know your PSAT scores. Record your test scores for easy reference.

Honors, awards, and prizes. Colleges want to see how you have been recognized in your school and community. List the academic honors that you have received as well as awards for being an outstanding artist or violinist and prizes for winning speech or 4-H contests.

Extracurricular activities. Colleges aren't just interested in your grades—they want to know what you have done in the areas of the arts, music, and athletics. They also want to know about your community and public service activities. Be specific in this section. List your best times if you are a swimmer or a runner. State that you played first chair in the violin section of your school orchestra. Tell what your responsibilities were as a hospital volunteer.

Employment. Schools like to know how much time you have spent working. Not only does it tell them about your work experience, it also explains why you may not have participated in extracurricular activities.

Travel experiences. This is the place to note trips to Washington, D.C., other states, and foreign countries.

Lessons. Colleges are interested in knowing about your special skills. Include your lessons on cooking, karate, and guitar in this section.

Books. Keep a record of all the books you have read during your high school years. Some colleges will want this information.

Use the next pages in this book to make a record of what you have done in high school.

Record of Subjects and Grades

Keep track of your grades here. At the end of each semester, write down the exact course title for each subject and your semester grade. Include all summer school courses in this record.

Ninth Grade			Tenth Grade		
Course title	Fall semester grade	Spring semester grade	Course title	Fall semester grade	Spring semester grade
1. _____			1. _____		
2. _____			2. _____		
3. _____			3. _____		
4. _____			4. _____		
5. _____			5. _____		
6. _____			6. _____		
7. _____			7. _____		
8. _____		Summer school grade	8. _____		Summer school grade
_____			_____		

Eleventh Grade			Twelfth Grade		
Course title	Fall semester grade	Spring semester grade	Course title	Fall semester grade	Spring semester grade
1. _____			1. _____		
2. _____			2. _____		
3. _____			3. _____		
4. _____			4. _____		
5. _____			5. _____		
6. _____			6. _____		
7. _____			7. _____		
8. _____			8. _____		
		Summer school grade			Summer school grade
_____			_____		
_____			_____		

Record of College Entrance Test Scores

PSAT

Test date _____ Verbal score _____ Mathematics score _____

Test date _____ Verbal score _____ Mathematics score _____

SAT

Test date _____ Verbal score _____ Mathematics score ___ TSWE score _____

Test date _____ Verbal score _____ Mathematics score ___ TSWE score _____

Achievement Tests

Name of test   Score   Test date

_____   _____   _____

_____   _____   _____

_____   _____   _____

_____   _____   _____

ACT

Test date _____ Composite score _____

Test date _____ Composite score _____

Record of Honors, Awards, Prizes, and Activities

Use this page and the next one to keep a list of the honors, awards, and prizes you have received and the activities in which you have been involved during high school.

Honors, Awards, and Prizes

Honors, awards, and prizes	Year received				Description
	9	10	11	12	

Extracurricular Activities (except athletics)						
	Grade level				Approximate time spent	
Activity	9	10	11	12	Hours per week	Positions held

Athletics					
	Participation by grade				
Sport	9	10	11	12	Positions held, letters won, special distinctions

Notes on times, scoring records, and other important sports activities	
Year	Notes

Employment (including summer)

Job	Employer	Approximate dates of employment	Approximate number of hours spent per week

Travel Experiences

Places visited	Approximate dates	Purpose

Lessons

Skill areas	Approximate dates	Skill level

Books Read	
Ninth Grade	Tenth Grade

Eleventh Grade	Twelfth Grade

Timetable for Admissions Process

Preparation for college is a four-year job. Each year you will have different tasks which you must do in between writing papers, completing projects, studying for tests, doing your homework, participating in extracurricular activities, and working. You won't have too much to do during the ninth and tenth grades; however, there are important things that you must do almost every month during the eleventh and twelfth grades.

The college planning calendar that follows will help you organize your time so that the admissions process will run smoothly for you. The calendar lists the steps you should be taking every year. Read through the calendar for an entire school year at the start of the year to get an overview of what you will need to do. Then during the year check off each step as you complete it. If a step does not apply to you, check it off. For example, not all students need to take Achievement Tests, apply for financial aid, or visit colleges.

By following the college planning calendar, you will avoid leaving out any vital steps in the admissions process. Although you can complete all of the steps on the planning calendar on your own, you will find it easier to complete these steps with the help of your guidance counselor, parents, and friends. Discuss the steps with them. Their experience can help you.

Ninth grade

In four years you will be in college. This is the year to start thinking about your future. Investigate several possible careers. Find out what education each requires. This is also the year to work on developing good study habits and to establish a reading program that will help you improve your vocabulary.

August–September

_____ Make sure that your course selections meet the requirements for high school graduation and for the colleges you may wish to attend.

_____ Set up a permanent file for school records.

September–December

_____ Encourage your parents to attend back-to-school

night so they will become familiar with your class schedule, teachers, and school.

_____ Explore extracurricular activities and begin participating in one or more activities.

_____ Begin investigating possible careers.

_____ Set up a reading program to develop your vocabulary.

January

_____ Prepare for semester tests because colleges are interested in your grades.

_____ Make possible program changes for second semester.

January–May

_____ Discuss educational goals with your guidance counselor.

_____ Review your four-year plan of classes and select appropriate courses for the next school year.

_____ Prepare for second-semester tests.

June

_____ Complete your written record of ninth grade.

_____ Save samples of your work, newspaper clippings, and copies of your grades and place them in the permanent record you are keeping.

Summer

_____ Continue reading program.

Tenth grade During this year, you will need to start thinking more seriously about college. It is time to discuss financing your college education with your family and to select a few colleges that might interest you. It is also the time to begin concentrating on just a few activities so that you can make an important contribution in those activities. If you are just beginning to use this calendar, make sure that you have completed all of the steps that should have been taken in ninth grade so you won't miss any important step in the admissions process.

August–September

_____ Make sure that your course selections meet the requirements for high school graduation and for the colleges you may wish to attend.

_____ Discuss with your guidance counselor the advisability of taking the P-ACT+ or the PSAT this year.

September–December

_____ Take the P-ACT+ or the PSAT in October, if advised to do so.

_____ Visit the guidance office to find out about college representatives visiting your school, college entrance tests, and career information.

_____ Encourage your parents to attend back-to-school night so they will become familiar with your class schedule, teachers, and school.

_____ Begin to concentrate on a few extracurricular activities.

_____ Begin to consider possible careers.

_____ Follow your reading program to continue developing your vocabulary.

January

_____ Prepare for semester tests because colleges are interested in your grades.

_____ Make possible program changes for second semester.

January–May

_____ Become better acquainted with your guidance counselor.

_____ Review your college and career goals.

_____ Select courses for the next school year that are compatible with your goals.

_____ Prepare for second-semester tests.

June

_____ Complete your written record of tenth grade.

_____ Save samples of your work, newspaper clippings, and copies of your grades and place them in the permanent record you are keeping.

Summer

_____ Continue reading program.

_____ Visit colleges and take tours.

Eleventh grade   This is a very important and busy year in the college admissions process. You will be taking college entrance tests, narrowing your list of possible colleges, and talking to college representatives. You should also be assuming the role of leader in your extracurricular activities.

If you are just beginning to use this calendar, make sure that you have completed all of the steps that should have been taken in ninth and tenth grades so you won't miss any important steps in the admissions process. Blank spaces are provided for you to enter important dates like registration deadlines for tests, test dates, and visits of college representatives to your school.

August–September

_____ Make sure that your course selections meet the requirements for high school graduation and for the colleges you may wish to attend.

_____ Study college catalogs and guidebooks.

_____ Plan the necessary entrance tests for college. Enter the registration deadlines and test dates on this calendar.

_____ Check with your guidance counselor about taking the PSAT and register for the test.

_____ Attend college representative meetings to learn more about colleges you are considering.

_____ Find out what information your school has about colleges.

_____ Obtain a social security number as you will need it for college and financial aid applications.

_____ Make plans to follow your reading program.

_____ _____

_____ _____

October

_____ Take the PSAT.

_____ Encourage your parents to attend back-to-school night so they will become familiar with your class schedule, teachers, and school.

_____ Continue attending college representative meetings.

_____ Begin writing to colleges for information.

_____ Organize a filing system to keep information on individual colleges.

_____ _____

_____ _____

November

_____ Continue writing to colleges for information.

_____ Continue attending college representative meetings.

_____ Continue investigating career choices and begin to make tentative choices about careers.

_____ Make plans to visit several colleges.

_____ Discuss financing your college education with your parents.

_____ _____

_____ _____

December

_____ Discuss your PSAT scores with your guidance counselor and use the scores to guide your college plans.

_____ Visit colleges you are interested in during your vacation.

_____ _____

_____ _____

January

_____ Prepare for semester tests because colleges are interested in your grades.

_____ Make possible program changes for second semester.

_____ _____

_____ _____

January–May

_____ Review your four-year plan of classes. Pay close attention to courses that will be required for college entrance.

_____ Select courses for the next school year that are compatible with your college and career goals.

_____ Reduce number of colleges that interest you.

_____ Write for information and applications from colleges that definitely interest you.

_____ Visit colleges for admissions interviews and tours.

_____ Talk to your guidance counselor about applying to colleges.

_____ Prepare individually or take a course to prepare for college admissions tests.

_____ Arrange to take the ACT or SAT on appropriate dates.

_____ Take Achievement Tests, if appropriate.

_____ Take advanced placement tests for AP courses you are completing.

_____ Preparc for second-semester tests.

_____ _____

_____ _____

June

_____ Take ACT, SAT, or Achievement Tests, if appropriate.

_____ Make plans to visit colleges during the summer.

_____ Complete your written record of your junior year.

_____ Save samples of your work, newspaper clippings, and copies of your grades.

Summer

_____ Continue reading program.

_____ Prepare for ACT or SAT, if necessary.

_____ Visit colleges for admissions interviews and tours.

_____ Complete application forms for colleges with early deadlines.

_____ Complete housing applications, if appropriate.

_____ _____

_____ _____

Twelfth grade   This is the year you must pull everything together. You should be taking challenging courses and playing an important role in extracurricular activities at your high school. Not only will you be busy with the demands of having a successful senior year, you will also be faced with the task of completing college applications and quite possibly taking the ACT, SAT, Achievement Tests, and AP examinations.

Before you look over this year's calendar, make sure that you have completed all the important steps listed on the calendars for previous years. Be sure to use the blank spaces on your senior calendar to list the various deadlines that you must meet.

August–September

_____ Make sure that your course selections meet the requirements for high school graduation and for the colleges you may wish to attend.

_____ Decide on final list of colleges to which you will apply.

_____ Obtain application forms from all colleges where you will apply for admission, if you haven't already done so.

_____ Work on college applications.

_____ Visit colleges for admissions interviews and tours.

_____ Talk to college representatives who visit your high school.

_____ Decide on test dates if you will be taking the ACT, SAT, or Achievement Tests.

_____ Make plans to prepare for any tests you will be taking.

_____ Investigate scholarship opportunities.

_____ Make sure you have written down all college application deadlines and test registration deadlines and dates.

_____ _____

_____ _____

October

_____ Complete all college applications with early deadlines.

_____ Take the ACT, if necessary.

_____ Prepare for any tests you will be taking.

_____ Give forms to people who will be writing letters of recommendation for you.

_____ Work on college applications and essays.

_____ Visit colleges for admissions interviews and tours.

_____ Encourage your parents to attend back-to-school nights, college nights, and financial aid nights.

_____ _____

_____ _____

November

_____ Obtain financial aid forms, if appropriate.

_____ Complete all applications.

_____ Take the SAT or Achievement Tests, if necessary.

_____ Visit colleges for admissions interviews and tours.

_____ _____

_____ _____

December

_____ Complete any applications that were not finished earlier.

_____ Start preparing financial aid forms.

_____ Visit colleges for admissions interviews and tours.

_____ Take the ACT, SAT, or Achievement Tests, if necessary.

_____ _____

_____ _____

January

_____ Prepare for semester tests because colleges are interested in your grades.

_____ Make any necessary schedule changes for second semester.

_____ Make final college visits and admissions interviews.

_____ Take SAT and Achievement Tests, if necessary.

_____ Send in all your college applications.

_____ Make sure all recommendations, transcripts, and test scores have been sent to each college.

_____ Send in financial aid forms.

_____ _____

_____ _____

February–April

_____ Make arrangements to take ACT in February and AP test in May, if necessary.

_____ Evaluate choices as you receive admissions decisions from colleges.

_____ Visit colleges to help you make your final decision.

_____   _____

_____   _____

May

_____   Notify colleges whether you are going to accept or
reject offers of admission.

_____   Take AP tests, if appropriate.

_____   Study for semester tests.

_____   Make sure a transcript of your final grades and
proof of graduation is sent to the college you will
be attending.

_____   _____

_____   _____

May–August

_____   Keep all material sent to you by the college that
you will be attending.

_____   Thank everyone who has helped you be admitted
to college.

_____   _____

_____   _____

Eliminating the Stress   Your mother wants you to attend the huge state university
because she was a cheerleader there while you would pre-
fer to go to a small college that doesn't even have a football
team. Your guidance counselor has just told you that you
should take the SAT again. You can't think of an essay
that is so innovative that it will scream, "Admit me!" Perhaps none of these things will happen to you. However, trying to get into college can be quite stressful. Very few students go through the college admissions process without
feeling some stress.

It is not possible to take all of the stress out of the admissions process, but it can be reduced if you follow the

steps on the college planning calendar. It spreads all the things you have to do to be admitted to college over four years. Even if you wait until you are a junior before you start thinking seriously about going to college, there is still time to do most of the things you should do without feeling too much pressure. When the college admissions process is organized and you don't feel rushed, you are likely to make the best possible choice of college for yourself—a decision that will affect many things that you do in the future.

Taking the College Admissions Tests

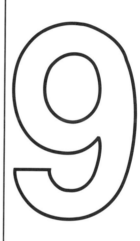

Do your admissions test scores really matter? The answer is "yes" at most four-year colleges. Of course grades, extracurricular activities, recommendations, essays, and work experiences also matter. But at many colleges, grades and test scores are the major factors in determining whether you will be accepted.

Colleges use admissions tests because the tests let them compare students across the nation to one standard. High school grading standards can vary enormously. Receiving a B in geometry at your high school with demanding Mr. Smith may have been a far greater achievement than an A with easy-going Ms. Jones at another school or even another teacher at your own school. In the same way, courses with identical names can vary considerably in difficulty between schools. Colleges can't tell these things by just looking at your grades and the courses you have taken.

Because college admissions tests can play an important

role in the admissions process, many students become absolutely terror stricken when they think of taking the SAT, ACT, or Achievement Tests. They forget that they have probably taken hundreds of tests and done well on them since the day they started school. In fact, most students who are applying to four-year colleges are actually experienced test takers. All they have to do to handle these tests is to approach them in the same way that they would any important test at their high schools. This means they need to know what these tests are like and then prepare for them.

In this chapter, you will find out what admissions tests are like and how to prepare for them. You will also learn some techniques to use in taking these tests, what your test scores mean, and when and how many times you should take these tests.

Finding Out about Admissions Tests

There is absolutely no mystery to what college admissions tests are like, for you can read a booklet describing each and every test. The booklets will tell you exactly what type of questions to expect and how many questions there will be of each type. Furthermore, there will be sample test questions or even sample tests. You can obtain these booklets from the guidance or career office at your high school.

Most students applying to four-year colleges will take either the Scholastic Aptitude Test (SAT) or the American College Test (ACT). For admission to some colleges, students will also be required to take Achievement Tests. You should check the test requirements of the colleges where you are thinking of applying before registering to take any of the tests. Many students take the Preliminary Scholastic Aptitude/National Merit Scholarship Qualifying Test (PSAT/NMSQT) or the P-ACT+ before taking the SAT or ACT. The more you know about all of these tests, the better you will do on them.

P-ACT+: a counseling tool

The P-ACT+ is given every October to sophomores. The purpose of the test is to help tenth graders determine their areas of academic weakness and strength so they can begin planning for their futures, including college admission. The P-ACT+ lets them see where they may need to strengthen their academic preparation. Although the test has the same multiple choice format as the ACT and covers the same high school curriculum areas, it is considered primarily a counseling tool rather than a practice test for the ACT.

PSAT/NMSQT: preparation for the SAT

In addition to being almost impossible to say, the PSAT/NMSQT is a multiple choice test composed of verbal and math sections like the SAT. Within each section the questions are similar to those you will find on the SAT. Each section has a score range from 20 to 80. Add a zero to your PSAT score, and it will correspond to SAT scoring. A score of 43 Verbal is equivalent to 430 on the SAT while a 55 Math is equivalent to 550. These scores are reported to you, your high school, and to certain scholarship agencies. They are not sent to colleges. However, some colleges will accept PSAT scores as admissions test scores.

There are several reasons for taking the PSAT/NMSQT, which is given only in October. First, it lets students see what objective admissions tests, especially the SAT, are like. Second, it gives students an idea of how well they will do on the SAT, which is helpful in making plans for college. Third, it is the qualifying test for scholarships from the National Merit Scholarship Corporation. Furthermore, if you are black, you may qualify for the National Achievement Scholarship Program for Outstanding Negro Students. And Hispanics taking the test become eligible for the College Board's National Hispanic Scholar Awards Program.

In December, you and your school receive the reports on your PSAT scores. This is important information. Spend time analyzing where you have made mistakes and which sections are giving you trouble so that you can work on these areas before taking the SAT.

The SAT: the major college entrance test

The SAT is not an intelligence test. It is primarily a multiple choice test of your verbal and mathematical abilities. When you take the SAT, you will have to complete two verbal sections of 85 questions, two mathematical sections of 60 questions, the Test of Standard Written English (TSWE) of 50 questions, and an equating section of either verbal, math, or TSWE questions. You will have 30 minutes to work on each section of the test.

The SAT scores that colleges consider are only the scores for the verbal and mathematical sections. The scores from the TSWE are used by colleges for placement in the appropriate English courses. The equating section is not scored. Its purpose is to test future SAT questions and to determine whether the test you are taking is harder or easier than past tests.

What's the SAT like? There is no better way to familiarize yourself with the SAT than by answering sample SAT questions and taking sample SAT tests. Learn more about the SAT by obtaining the booklet entitled *Taking the SAT,* which is published by the College Board. Most high schools distribute the booklet free of charge to students. It is also available for a nominal fee by writing to: College Board ATP, P.O. Box 6200, Princeton, NJ 08541-6200.

The ACT Assessment   The official name of the other major college admissions test is the ACT Assessment, but most people simply call it the ACT. Although both the ACT and the SAT are multiple choice tests, they are definitely not identical tests. They test different things. While the SAT has verbal and math tests, the ACT consists of four tests: English, mathematics, reading, and science reasoning.

The ACT and SAT have very different scoring systems. When you get your ACT test results, you receive scores and subscores for each test as well as a composite score for the entire test. Each of the four test scores and the total composite score have a range of 1 to 36.

Learn about the ACT. Become better acquainted with the ACT by answering sample items for the English, mathematics, reading, and science reasoning tests. You can do this by picking up a copy of the booklet *Preparing for the ACT Assessment,* which should be available through the counseling office at your high school.

The Achievement Tests   Achievement Tests aren't like the SAT and the ACT. They are tests of your knowledge or skills in different subjects. Altogether there are fourteen Achievement Tests which fall into five general subject areas:

- English
  English Composition (two versions)
  Literature

- Foreign Languages
  French
  German
  Hebrew
  Latin
  Spanish

- History and Social Studies
  American History and Social Studies
  European History and World Culture

- Mathematics
  Mathematics Level I
  Mathematics Level II

- Sciences
  Biology
  Chemistry
  Physics

The Achievement Tests are given on five dates during the school year; however, not all tests are given on each date. All the tests take one hour of testing time, and you can take as many as three tests on any one test date. All of the tests are multiple choice except for the English Composition Test with Essay, which has an essay as well as multiple choice questions. This test is given only in December.

The more selective a college is, the more likely you will have to take Achievement Tests. Some colleges request that you take one or two specific tests, usually the English Composition and the Mathematics tests. Others let you choose the tests that you prefer. You will probably do better on an Achievement Test if you take it soon after completing a course in the subject while the material is still fresh in your mind. For that reason, June can be an excellent month to take Achievement Tests. If you haven't studied a subject recently, you should always review it thoroughly before taking an Achievement Test.

Look at Achievement Tests. Never choose the Achievement Tests you will take without looking at samples in several subject areas. You may find the questions in one subject area to be much easier than another. Be sure also to look closely at the two Mathematics Tests to determine which level is most appropriate. And think carefully about whether you will do better on the English Composition Test with or without essay.

Admissions Tests Require Careful Timing

Without some advance planning of your testing schedule, disaster may occur. You may find that you don't have time to study for a required Achievement Test or to retake the SAT when your score is lower than you wanted. You may also find you have to take a test the same day as the state cross country meet or your brother's wedding.

Test-wise students don't wait until their senior year to begin taking admissions tests. Students planning to take the ACT take the P-ACT+ as sophomores and the ACT as juniors. Students can take the PSAT as sophomores, but most wait until they are juniors to take this test. Then in the spring of their junior year, they take the SAT so that they will have time to retake the test, if necessary. Knowing what their test scores are on the ACT or SAT at an early date helps students choose the colleges to which they will apply. Test-wise students also take Achievement Tests shortly after completing a course. This could mean taking the Achievement Test in a subject like biology as early as May or June of your sophomore year.

Planning your test schedule

The first step in planning your test schedule is to know which admissions tests the colleges you are seriously considering want you to take. If you have a choice between taking the ACT or SAT, study each test bulletin carefully. Then take the sample tests to discover on which test you can do the best. Do the same thing to decide which Achievement Tests you will take if you can choose these tests. Some Achievement Tests may seem much easier to you than others.

Complete the following chart so that you will have a clear picture of which college admissions tests you will need to take.

Tests Required for Admission to College

Name of College	ACT or SAT (required)	Names of Achievement Tests (if required)		
		_____	_____	_____
		_____	_____	_____
		_____	_____	_____
		_____	_____	_____
		_____	_____	_____

Choosing your test dates. Each year the ACT, SAT, and Achievement Tests are given in the same months. It is possible to take the ACT and the SAT or Achievement Tests in the same month but not the SAT and Achievement Tests. Use the information in the following table to decide when you will take each test.

Schedule of Test Dates

Test Dates	Test Given
October*	SAT, ACT
November	SAT, Ach
December	SAT, Ach, ACT
January	SAT, Ach
February**	ACT
March/April***	SAT, ACT
May	SAT, Ach
June	SAT, Ach, ACT

*The SAT is given only in California, Georgia, Hawaii, Illinois, North Carolina, South Carolina, and Texas.
**The ACT is not given in New York on this date.
***Whether this test date is in March or April varies.

Creating your own test schedule. You need to consider the following points in planning your own test schedule:

- You cannot take the SAT and Achievement Tests on the same day.

- You may want to take the ACT or SAT more than once.

- You can take only three Achievement Tests in a test session.

- You must consider which Achievement Tests are given on each date.

- Colleges have certain deadlines for receiving test scores.

- It is helpful to have time to prepare for admissions tests.

In order to complete your personal test schedule, you will have to look at test registration booklets to determine the actual test dates and registration deadlines. Once your schedule is complete, be sure to write all the test and registration dates on your planning calendar.

Student's Test Schedule

Name of Test	Test Date	Registration Deadline

Registering for Tests   You will find all the information you need about registering for tests in the registration bulletins put out for the ACT, the SAT, and Achievement Tests. When you fill in the registration forms, you must be sure that you use the same name that you are going to use on all your college applications in order to avoid confusion later on. You also need to know your social security number and your high school code number which is on test posters at your school or available at the career or guidance office. Write this information down now so you can use it when registering for tests:

Last Name   First Name   Middle Initial

_____

Social Security Number __ __ __ - __ __ - __ __ __ __

Your High School Code __ __ __ - __ __ __

A free information service. When you are filling in the registration form for the ACT or the SAT, you can indicate that you want certain information about yourself sent to colleges, governmental agencies, and scholarship agencies. If you do, you may be deluged in mail from colleges that are interested in having students like you.

Test questions and answers. For certain test dates you can get a copy of the test you took, your answers, and the correct answers. This is helpful information if you plan to retake a test.

Registration deadlines. If you should miss a registration deadline or suddenly decide to take a test, all of the tests have late registration dates. You may even be able to take the SAT or Achievement Tests as a standby.

Your admission ticket. You should receive an admission ticket well before each test. Be sure to contact the testing agency if you have not received your ticket before the time stated in the registration bulletin. When you receive your ticket, make sure that all of the following information is accurate: your name, sex, birthdate, social security number, telephone number, name of the test, test date, and test center. If not, follow instructions to correct or add information.

How to Prepare for Admissions Tests

Even if you are a straight-A student who aces every test, you will probably do better on college admissions tests by spending some time in preparing for them. The bare minimum of preparation for these tests is to read test bulletins. In fact, you should read these bulletins several times because they provide so much helpful information.

Reading a test bulletin will help you become familiar with the content and organization of a test and will provide you with test-taking tips. If you don't read a bulletin before taking a test, you simply won't know what to expect on the test. Furthermore, everything that you see on the test you will be seeing for the first time—a serious disadvantage.

Practice with actual tests

The more familiar you are with the format of a test, the less anxious you will feel about taking it. Besides, when you are familiar with a test, you can devote all of your time to answering the questions rather than worrying about understanding the directions. The best way to become familiar with a test is by practicing on actual tests that have been given in years past. The College Board publishes several books of sample tests, which are available from your school guidance or career office, your school or local library, and in bookstores. In the fall of 1989, the ACT began administering a redesigned test that is not the same as earlier tests. Consult the ACT registration bulletin for information about obtaining sample tests.

When you work with practice tests, it is important to take a number of them under the same time limits you will have on the test day. This will teach you how to pace yourself on the test.

Preparing for the SAT

There has been a great amount of controversy over how to prepare for the SAT. Some feel the answer lies in getting coaching while others favor vocabulary-building programs, extensive reading, doing well in your classes, or using preparation guides and computer programs. All of these things can be helpful. How successful any form of preparation will be depends largely on your motivation to improve your vocabulary and math skills, because that is what the SAT is all about. When students work hard in these two areas for weeks before a test, they will do better on the SAT.

One thing is certain—the experts agree that cramming right before the test is rarely going to result in significantly higher scores. And that, of course, is what preparation is all about—getting the highest possible scores you are able to get.

Vocabulary-building programs. The verbal part of the SAT is based almost entirely on vocabulary. The larger your vocabulary, the better you will do. The most effective way to build your vocabulary is by reading, reading, and more reading. In chapter 4, it was suggested that you start a reading program when you enter high school. Even if you haven't been much of a reader, extensive reading in your junior year can improve your vocabulary and comprehension skills. You can also improve your vocabulary by working with vocabulary lists that contain words frequently found on the SAT.

Preparation books and computer programs. By working alone with SAT preparation books and computer programs, students can become more familiar with the test format as well as increase their math and vocabulary skills. Some students like the immediate feedback offered by computer programs which lets them see at once whether or not an answer is correct as well as the reasoning behind each answer.

Coaching courses. There is now agreement that coaching can improve test scores. The question is by how much, since this coaching can be quite expensive—hundreds of dollars. In general, the lower the score, the greater the improvement, provided a student really works hard. These courses do provide review, improve skills—especially math skills—give students practice in taking the test, and make students feel more comfortable about taking these tests.

Preparing for Achievement Tests

Since you will be tested on factual knowledge on the Achievement Tests, what you have learned in school plays a large role in these tests. You will get the best idea of what you need to know for any Achievement Test by studying sample tests. Then by taking sample tests, you will find out what your weaknesses are and can devote your time to reviewing these areas in your textbooks.

Ready, Set, Go—It's Test Time!

Give yourself the advantage of being organized for an admissions test. First of all, avert disaster on the morning of the test by making sure several days before the test where your test center is if it isn't in your own school. There are real horror stories about students who couldn't find a test center until after a test had started.

Don't turn the night before the test into an all-night cram session. Limit your time to reviewing what you have been studying. Then go to bed and set your alarm so you will have time to get up and leave for the test without a frantic Dagwood Bumstead exit.

Remember that getting off to a flying start on a test doesn't mean arriving with unsharpened pencils a minute before the test is to start. Here is your checklist of things to put in one spot the night before a test.

_____ your admission ticket

_____ four sharpened (soft-lead) no. 2 pencils and a very good eraser.

_____ identification that meets the requirements stated in the registration bulletin

_____ a watch, as test centers are not required to provide clocks

_____ a snack for your break

Test-taking strategies

Before you arrive at the test center to take an admissions test, your test-taking strategy should be set. By reading the test bulletin, you have learned specific test-taking tips that the testmaker believes will help you on the test. By doing practice tests, you know what the test is like and how to pace yourself to do your best.

There are only a few things left that you can do on the test day to ensure that the outcome is as successful as possible:

- Arrive early enough so you can choose the best possible seating. You don't want to be distracted because your chair is uncomfortable or you are sitting next to a heating or air-conditioning unit. Ask to be moved if it is necessary.

- When you receive your test, make sure that both the test booklet and answer sheet are complete and legible.

- When you run out of energy, have a piece of gum or candy available to recharge yourself.

- Check your answer sheet periodically to make sure that your answers are in the right place and sufficiently darkened.

- Be sure to erase any extraneous answers on the answer sheet as they can cause your test to be scored incorrectly.

After You Receive Your Scores

Don't panic if your scores on admissions tests are not as good as you wished. On the other hand, if they are great, don't assume that you will be admitted to the college of your dreams. Your test scores are only one part of the decision of a college to admit you.

What you want to do with your test scores is to evaluate whether they meet the requirements of the schools that interest you. State colleges tend to have a minimum or suggested score that students should meet while private schools tend to be more fuzzy about what their requirements are, listing only the average scores of recent classes. You can use the following chart to evaluate your test scores and determine if you will want to retake a test.

Possible Colleges	Suggested Scores			My Test Scores		
	ACT	SAT		ACT	SAT	
		V	M		V	M

Should you retake a test?

Some students should retake admissions tests. If your scores do not meet the requirements of a state school or are below the average scores of students accepted at a selective school, you need to retake a test. You should also consider retaking a test if you need a higher score for a possible scholarship. Students' scores usually go up the second time they take a test. There is very little reason, however, for students with exceptionally high scores to retake a test as they may not do as well the second time. You can, of course, retake admissions tests more than once.

Deciding Where You Will Apply to College

10

Where will you send your college applications? Is it to schools 5 or 1,500 miles from your home? Is it to your parents' alma maters or to the schools all your friends plan to attend? You are the person in charge of deciding where you will apply to college. This is one of the first big decisions that you will have to make in your life. It is, obviously, a very important decision. However, a lot of people—parents, counselors, friends, and college admissions officers—will give you valuable help.

There is no particularly scientific approach to selecting the colleges to which you will apply. In fact, part of the decision will depend on your own feelings about different schools. It doesn't make much sense to apply to a college because it has an excellent art department if you know you couldn't stand living where the college is located for more than a month.

In this chapter, you will find out about steps you can

take to make the job of deciding where to apply to college much easier. You will learn how to find out what different colleges offer, how to have successful campus visits and interviews, and how to narrow your selections to the schools that most closely match your abilities, needs, and goals.

Consider Your Goals

Think back now to the goals you listed as possible career choices in chapter 1. Were they definite choices or just fuzzy ideas about your future? Either answer affects your decision about where you should apply to college. For example, if you know that you definitely want to be an engineer, it only makes sense to apply to schools that offer degrees in engineering. And obviously students who want to devote all their time to the study of art or music should look for schools that will let them concentrate on those areas.

If you are not certain about what you would like to do in the future but think that it will be in a field like science or the liberal arts, you will need to apply to schools that offer those particular curriculums. And if you are very uncertain about your career goals, you will need to find schools that offer a very wide range of courses. You should also realize that for many careers you can get all the preparation that you need at a two-year technical or community college.

Choosing an academic program. Your first consideration in narrowing the list of colleges to which you will apply is to find colleges that offer the academic program that will allow you to achieve your career goals. So take the time right now to check what type of academic program you need.

_____ emphasis on liberal arts

_____ emphasis on science and math

_____ broad curriculum including liberal arts and science

_____ specialty school (art, drama, mining)

_____ technical college that stresses career education

Choosing a major. The field of study in which a student specializes and receives his or her degree is called a major. Some students know what their majors will be when they enter college, but most do not. Furthermore, many college students choose a major only to switch to another field later on. Nevertheless, if you feel strongly that you want to major in Japanese or architecture, make sure that you are applying to colleges that offer these majors. List the major or majors that interest you so you can consider them when applying to colleges:

Possible major or majors: _____

_____

Obtaining Information about Different Colleges

By deciding on the college academic program you want and a possible major or majors, you have set up guidelines that will reduce the number of colleges you need to contact for information. You can use directories like the following ones to determine which schools have the academic programs and majors you want:

> *Index of Majors,* College Entrance Examination Board

> *Barron's Profiles of American Colleges, Index of College Majors*

If there is one part to the admissions process that is easy to handle, it is obtaining information about colleges. In fact, good students will almost drown in the amount of material that will be sent to them. You will probably start getting mail from colleges as soon as you take one of the admissions tests if you checked the box on the registration form allowing information about yourself to be sent to different colleges. Here are some other ways to get information about colleges.

College directories

A good place to start looking for information is by studying one of the big college directories like *Barron's Profiles of American Colleges; Peterson's Guide to Four-Year Colleges;*

The College Handbook, College Board Publications; or *College Admissions Data Handbook,* Orchard House, Inc. You will find these directories and many others in libraries and bookstores and at your own high school in the library, guidance, or career office.

These directories have a wealth of factual information about such things as costs, admissions requirements, programs of study, financial aid, selectivity, student life, environment, and profiles of the freshman class.

College mailings   When you want more information about a particular college than you find in a directory, write the college and ask for it. If you want specific information about anything like a co-op program or scholarships, you must request it. Just a brief letter or a postcard like the following one is all you need to send to the college. Don't forget to include your name and address. You can get the school's mailing address from a directory.

Office of Admissions
Name of College
Address

I am currently a *(year in school)* at *(name of school)*. I am interested in receiving information about *(name of college)*. Please send me *(an application form, catalog, financial aid information and forms, or whatever specific information you want)*.

Thank you.

(Name) _____

(Address) _____

(City, State, ZIP) _____

Students asking for information from colleges are usually sent brochures or a viewbook. This information has attractive pictures of the campus, faculty, and students as well as information about entrance requirements and procedures, housing, social life, the faculty, course offerings, special programs like overseas study, athletic teams, and extracurricular activities. Because catalogs are expensive to produce, students will not often receive one unless they request it. Once you have written to a college and requested information, you should expect to continue receiving mail from that college.

Catalogs

College catalogs are not meant to be read from cover to cover but to be used to find out specific details about a school. Besides information about the school, admissions, policies, procedures, and the faculty, you will find descriptions of the courses and course requirements for different majors in a catalog. Instead of sending for a catalog, you can see catalogs or look at them on microfiche at many libraries and high school guidance or career offices.

Videos

Videos give you a sense of what a campus is like. They help you understand its life-style. On videos you can see students and faculty members talking about such things as course offerings, special programs, housing, sports, and extracurricular activities. In many ways, seeing a video is the next best thing to visiting a college campus. The place to find videos is in school and public libraries and high school guidance or career offices.

College representatives

Watch for the visits of college representatives to your high school. By attending a session with a visiting representative, you can learn two very important things: what a school is like and what type of students it wants. In addition, you can ask specific questions about the college and get expert answers.

College information nights and college fairs

By going to a college information night or a college fair, you have the chance to see what a great number of colleges from different areas of the country offer in a very short period of time. You can pick up college brochures, viewbooks, and catalogs and sign up for more material to be sent to you. You also have the chance to chat briefly with different college representatives.

Enlisting the computer's help

Computers can help you find colleges that have the features you want. Type in the characteristics you want, like size, cost, location, and a major in Russian history, and a list of colleges that meet your requirements will emerge on the printout. Then you can request additional information on what individual colleges are like and see the profile of a school. Many high schools and public libraries have computer software or terminals that will give you access to this information.

An overlooked source of information—people

Students often overlook getting information about different colleges from people they know. Quite often these people can give them a good picture of what college and college life are really like. Talking to people gives you the chance to add a personal touch to the information you are gathering about colleges. Have you talked to the following people about college?

- your parents
- brothers and sisters in college
- your high school guidance or career counselor
- older friends in college
- friends of your parents
- people working in careers that interest you
- alumni of a specific college

Private counselors. There are also private counselors who provide students with information about colleges and help students find colleges that match their interests and abilities. Some of these counselors also help students complete their applications. This type of counseling can be expensive. It is also very important to check the background of these counselors.

Making Your Tentative List of Colleges

Once you have some information about colleges, you are ready to make a tentative list of schools that you want to investigate further. You don't want to have too long a list—twenty is probably a maximum number—because you really want to learn what these colleges are like. You will read all you can about these schools, look at videos of them, and talk to people about them. Part of learning about these colleges will also include visiting some of them and having interviews at the colleges that truly interest you. Remember, this is not the final list of colleges to which you will actually apply but a list of colleges that interest you for a variety of reasons.

Organize information on colleges

You need to have some system to organize all the mailings you will receive from colleges and the information you pick up at college fairs, college nights, and the guidance office at your school. You don't have to have a sophisticated filing system to keep track of all the materials, but you should place all the material about one school in the same envelope or folder.

As you read through the material, you should sort it into at least three categories. The material from schools that do not meet your basic goals should simply be thrown out. The rest of the material can be divided into two categories: schools that really interest you and schools in which you may have some interest.

Your tentative list

Put on your tentative list of schools all those with materials that you placed in the "schools that really interest you" category. Add the schools that you have always thought about attending. Then add the schools that your parents think are good choices for you. Don't forget to put a state college or university on your list. Finally, if you have room on your list, you can also add schools that friends, relatives, and counselors have recommended to you. You can also add schools that you filed in the "have some interest" category.

Check your list. You may need to add or subtract some schools. You want to have a realistic list that offers you a number of options. You should be able to answer "yes" to all of the following questions about your tentative list:

1. Are there schools on the list where you will definitely be admitted? _____ (Many colleges,

including some state schools, admit all high school graduates.)

2. Are there schools on the list where you are likely to be admitted because your grades and test scores meet the minimum entrance requirements? _____

3. Are there schools on your list whose admissions requirements are a reach for your qualifications? _____ (Outstanding strengths in extracurricular activities can sometimes lead to admission to schools where students' grades and test scores are below the usual entrance requirements.)

4. Are most of the schools on your list ones that you can afford? _____ (Financial aid is discussed in chapter 12.)

5. Do all the schools on your list meet your academic program and career requirements? _____

Reduce your list to twenty schools. If your tentative list is too large, reduce it by finding out more about individual schools so you can select those that are most appealing to you in such areas as course offerings, location, environment, and cost. Then write your list of tentative schools in the space provided. The list of schools that you visit and to which you apply should come from this group of colleges.

Tentative List of Schools

1. _____   8. _____   15. _____

2. _____   9. _____   16. _____

3. _____   10. _____   17. _____

4. _____   11. _____   18. _____

5. _____   12. _____   19. _____

6. _____   13. _____   20. _____

7. _____   14. _____

Visiting Colleges That Interest You

You can look at pictures in brochures and viewbooks and read campus profiles in directories and even see videos of campuses, but it is not the same as walking around a campus, talking to students and faculty members, and spending a night in a dorm. By visiting a campus, you really can tell what a college is like and whether it is the right one for you. Visits also let you compare the subtle differences between colleges, which is very helpful in deciding to which colleges you will apply. Of course, you won't be able to visit all of the schools on your tentative list, but you should try to visit the most appealing ones.

The time to visit colleges

Most students will visit colleges in the spring of their junior year, the summer before their senior year, or in the fall of their senior year. Visits to several colleges can be part of a family vacation. You can also visit colleges when they hold special preview or college days for high school students. A casual visit to a nearby campus should be made sometime during the first two years of high school. Such a visit can be very motivational, giving a student a solid reason to do better academically or to shine in extracurricular activities. It is decidedly helpful to have visited a campus before applying for admission.

The best time to visit a college is during the week when school is in session. Try to avoid finals week or a big game weekend so that you can get a picture of everyday campus life. While admissions officers have more time to talk to you in the summer, the disadvantage is that there may be few or no students on campus.

The more time you can spend on a campus, the better you will be able to tell what a college is like. Ideally, you should spend a day and a night at a school. By spending a night, especially a weeknight, you can get a good idea of how much studying, talking, and partying the students do at night and how it fits with your life-style.

Preparing for a college visit

Students, not their parents, should do most of the preparation for college visits. This includes contacting the admissions office for an interview, finding out the times of campus tours and group information sessions, and making arrangements to stay overnight in a dorm. If you have special interests that you definitely want to pursue in college, you should mention this to the admissions office before you arrive on campus. The office may be able to arrange for you to visit classes, talk to faculty members, or visit with coaches and students. Preparing for a visit also includes studying up on a school so you know what you want to see and what questions you want answered.

What to see and do   Colleges want to interest visiting students in applying and enrolling in their schools. Most schools have well-organized tours that show off their schools. Many also have group information sessions where students can learn about academic programs, housing, social life, and admissions as well as ask questions. Students can get a good picture of a school in a limited amount of time by going on a tour and attending a group information session.

Begin your college visit at the admissions office where you can join tours or group information sessions or if necessary pick up a map for a self-guided tour. How much you can see and do during a visit naturally depends on how much time you are able to spend on the campus. To have a good campus visit you should at least do the following things:

- Take a tour of the campus, which includes seeing classrooms, the library, the student union, and student housing.

- Attend a group information session.

- Pick up a copy of the student newspaper.

- Visit the financial aid office for applications and information if you will be applying for aid.

Students who plan on spending a full day at a college will want to add the following activities to their list so they can become even better acquainted with a school:

- Sit in on at least one class in an area that interests them.

- Have a meal in a campus dining hall.

- Find out where students can find a snack when they are tired of dorm food.

- Talk to students about what the school is like.

- Talk to faculty members to learn more about programs that interest them.

- Talk to coaches if they want to participate in sports on the varsity level.

- Talk to students involved in extracurricular activities that they would like to pursue on campus.

- Wander around the school just absorbing the atmosphere.

Once you have visited a college, take a few minutes to jot down your reactions to the school. If you meet any people whom you would like to contact for more information, be sure to write down their names.

Having a Successful Interview

There are two excellent reasons for scheduling a college interview. First, it is an opportunity for students to become real people to admissions officers instead of a combination of grades, scores, and activities on an application. Second, it lets students learn more about a college.

The importance of the interview in the admissions process varies enormously. It is certainly not the most important factor in a student being admitted to a college. Some colleges don't even hold interviews, and others don't put interview notes in students' files. However, at some schools an interview can make a difference in a student being admitted or not being admitted to the college. You can't change your grades or scores, but a good interview can make you a more attractive admissions prospect to a school. This is especially true if you are applying to a selective school and are not at the top of the list for admission.

When to schedule an interview

It helps to schedule an interview after a campus tour because you are then more familiar with what the college is like and able to ask better questions. You should call to schedule an interview rather than write because you may have to juggle dates to find an interview time, especially in the fall, which is when most high school seniors schedule their interviews. Saturday morning is usually the most popular time. For very selective schools, it is probably a good idea to schedule an interview as much as two months in advance of your proposed date to visit a college. Because interviewers are so rushed in the fall, interviews in the spring of your junior year or summer before your senior year may be longer and easier to arrange. Try to schedule interviews at schools where you really want to be accepted after you have interviewed at other schools so you will be more experienced with the interviewing process.

Rules for a successful interview

College admissions officers agree that there are certain basic rules that must be followed in order to have a successful interview:

- Be prepared.

- Take your interview confirmation ticket.

- Arrive early for your interview.

- Dress conservatively.

- Leave your parents in the waiting room.

- Participate actively in the interview.

- Be yourself.

- Send a thank-you note.

How to prepare for the interview

Unless you have read the school brochures and viewbooks from cover to cover, you simply won't have the basic information about a school that you need for an interview. Interviewers are not impressed with students when an entire interview is spent discussing information about the college that the student should have known from doing some reading about the school. It also helps to have toured the campus before your interview so that you have a better feel of the school's atmosphere.

Prepare to answer basic questions. No matter where you interview, the interviewer is quite likely to ask questions about the type of person you are, your values and goals, and your reasons for wanting to attend that college. If you haven't given some thought to these areas, you may stumble with your answers. Since you may be asked the following questions at every interview, take the time now to write down how you will answer them. There are no right or wrong answers to these questions; however, you want to show interviewers that you have spent some time thinking about these basic questions.

1. Why do you want to attend this college?

_____

_____

_____

_____

_____

_____

_____

_____

_____

_____

2. What are you thinking of as a possible major? Why?

_____

_____

_____

_____

_____

_____

_____

_____

_____

3. What do you see yourself doing in the future? Five years from now? Ten years from now?

_____

_____

_____

_____

_____

_____

_____

_____

_____

_____

4. What are your most important contributions to your high school?

_____

_____

_____

_____

_____

_____

_____

_____

_____

5. How would you describe yourself to a stranger? (Use lots of adjectives.)

_____

_____

_____

_____

_____

_____

_____

_____

_____

Expect to answer some of these questions. As the interviewer gets to know you better, you may be asked many questions like the following ones. Thinking about your answers before the interview will make you feel more relaxed at the interview.

College

1. Where else are you applying to college?

2. What do you feel you have to offer this college?

3. What do you expect to get out of a college education?

4. What extracurricular activities do you plan to pursue in college?

High School

1. Which subject have you liked best or least in high school?

2. How demanding is your high school?

3. What would you like to change about your high school?

4. What is your favorite teacher like?

Yourself

1. How would your teachers or friends describe you?

2. What are your greatest strengths or weaknesses?

3. Who are your heroes? Why?

4. What books have you read this year?

Anticipate some unusual questions. Some interviewers like to see how you can handle something out of the ordinary. How you answer unusual questions is less important than your ability not to be flustered by them. What would you reply to these questions?

1. How would you spend $1 million in 24 hours?

2. Would you rather be an elephant or a mouse?

Have some questions of your own. Sometime during the interview the interviewer will ask if you have any questions. You want to ask questions that reveal how seriously you are interested in the school rather than ones that could be answered by reading the college brochure. Ask, "Is it possible to have a double major in psychology and history?" Don't ask, "Is there a psychology department?"

Write down three questions now that you would like to ask at the interview. Then take them with you to the interview in case your mind goes blank.

1. _____

_____

_____

2. _____
    _____
    _____

3. _____
    _____
    _____

What to expect   When you arrive at the admissions office for your interview, it will be crowded with other prospective students and their parents. You need to sign in and take a seat. Your interviewer will come into the office and call your name. You need to stand up at once so the interviewer will know who you are. Greet the interviewer with a handshake and introduce anyone who is with you.

Your interview will last from 20 to 45 minutes. The length of time is more dependent on the interviewer's schedule than the way you have impressed the interviewer. It will usually begin with break-the-ice clichés like a discussion of your trip to the college. The rest of the interview will be devoted to the interviewer's questions and your questions. At the end of the interview, express your appreciation for the opportunity to learn more about the school. Be sure to learn the interviewer's name, because you will want to write a letter repeating how you valued the interview and mentioning something that was discussed to remind the interviewer of you.

Alumni interviews   Some selective colleges require alumni interviews. Others strongly recommend alumni interviews. These interviews can take the place of on-campus interviews when it is impossible for students to visit a school. Many students have both on-campus and alumni interviews. Like on-campus interviews, alumni interviews are an opportunity for students to learn more about a college and to have additional information about themselves put in their admissions folders. Students should prepare for these interviews in the same way they do for on-campus interviews.

Narrowing Your Choices

Once information on colleges has been gathered from directories, brochures, viewbooks and guidebooks, interviews and campus tours, students are ready to narrow their choices of colleges. They need to evaluate what they know about different colleges and then decide where they want to go to college and apply to those schools. In order to do this they have to figure out exactly what they want in a college. Answering the following questions will give you a better idea of what your preferences are. Then you can determine which colleges match your preferences most closely.

Location

1. Where would you like to go to college?

   a. the East

   b. the Midwest

   c. the South

   d. the Southwest

   e. the West

2. Where would you prefer to live while you are in college?

   a. a metropolitan area

   b. a large city

   c. the suburbs

   d. a small town

   e. a rural area

Write down the colleges on your tentative list that most closely match where you would like to live.

_____   _____   _____

_____   _____   _____

_____   _____   _____

_____   _____   _____

College environment

1. What type of school would you like to attend?

    a. single sex

    b. coeducational

2. What size student body most appeals to you?

    a. less than 1,500 students

    b. 1,500 to 3,000 students

    c. 3,000 to 5,000 students

    d. 5,000 to 10,000 students

    e. more than 10,000 students

3. What type of living arrangements would you prefer?

    a. on-campus dormitory

    b. sorority or fraternity

    c. off campus

    d. live at home

    e. other _____

4. What type of campus activities would you like?

    a. a wide variety of extracurricular activities

    b. a broad athletic program

    c. a lively social life

    d. a strong focus on religion

    e. other _____

    f. some combination of a,b,c,d,e (circle choices)

Write down the colleges on your tentative list that most closely match the college environment you are seeking.

_____   _____   _____

_____   _____   _____

_____   _____   _____

Academic Offerings and Facilities

1. What types of programs do you want a college to offer?
   a. co-op program (work/study)
   b. overseas study
   c. internships
   d. other _____
   e. some combination of a,b,c,d,e (circle choices)
2. What facilities at a college are important to you?
   a. number of computer terminals
   b. number of volumes in the library
   c. student union
   d. sports facilities
   e. other _____
   f. some combination of a,b,c,d,e (circle choices)

Write down the colleges on your tentative list that most closely match the academic offerings and facilities you want.

_____   _____   _____

_____   _____   _____

_____   _____   _____

Finalizing your list   Once you know what you are looking for in a college, decide which factors are most important to you. Is it going to a school in the Midwest? Is it a junior-year-abroad program? Is it attending a small school in a rural setting? Narrow your tentative list of colleges further by eliminating all the schools that don't have what you really want to find in a college. Then compare the remaining colleges on your list until you come up with five to ten colleges that you would really like to attend. Write this list down.

List of Preferred Schools

1. _____   6. _____

2. _____   7. _____

3. _____   8. _____

4. _____   9. _____

5. _____   10. _____

Cost. You can't finalize the list of colleges to which you will apply until you have considered if you will be able to afford the schools. Going to college can be very expensive. Some selective private schools now cost more than $20,000 a year to attend, and state-supported schools can cost over $5000 for just tuition and room and board. Use the financial information found in college profiles in directories to determine what the colleges on your list will cost to attend and how much the typical financial aid package is worth.

College Costs

Name of College	Tuition	Room and Board	Total*	Typical Aid Package

*Total does not include books, transportation, or personal expenses.

Even though college is expensive and becoming more expensive each year, financial aid makes it possible for most college applicants to attend college. The majority of students at almost all colleges are receiving some kind of financial aid. While directories give information only about typical aid packages, students can receive considerably more or less than this amount. You must also realize that few financial aid packages cover the entire cost of college. Chapter 12 includes a discussion of ways to obtain financial aid.

Students need to have frank talks with their parents about how much their parents can contribute to their education before finalizing their list of college choices. They may need to include more schools that they can afford on their preferred list. Students also need to investigate fully all the options available for financial help in getting the education they want. This is why it is a good idea to include a visit to the financial aid office at every college that you tour.

Selectivity. Some schools will admit all high school graduates while others are so selective that only 16 percent of those who apply are admitted. Determine how your grades and test scores compare to those required for schools on your preferred list.

Admissions Requirements

Name of College	Required GPA*	My GPA	Minimum			My Scores		
			SAT		ACT	SAT		ACT
			V	M		V	M	

*GPA—grade point average

Arrange the schools on your preferred list in three groups to reflect the difficulty you will encounter in being admitted to those schools. In the first group, place those schools that are "sure admissions" because your grades and test scores are well above the minimum required for those schools. In the second group, list the colleges that are "probable admissions" since the average grades and test scores of those admitted are similar to yours. And finally, put in the third group those schools at which you only stand a chance of being admitted. You should have at least one school in each group.

Selectivity List

Sure Admissions	Probable Admissions	Uncertain Admissions
_____	_____	_____
_____	_____	_____
_____	_____	_____
_____	_____	_____
_____	_____	_____

Your final choices

How many colleges should you apply to? There is no right number. For most students, the right answer is probably somewhere between three and seven schools. Students should apply to more than one school because acceptance is not always a certainty and it is good to have a choice.

Choose the final list of schools that you would most like to attend and to which you will apply from your selectivity list. Make sure that you choose at least one school in the "sure admissions" category. It is also a good idea to reach a little, so put at least one school from the "uncertain" category on your final list. Finally, choose your favorites from the "probable" category. Then write down the names of the colleges, listing them by first to last choice.

Final College Admissions Choices

1. _____   5. _____

2. _____   6. _____

3. _____   7. _____

4. _____

Now that you have carefully selected the schools to which you will apply, you are ready to begin filling out your applications.

Filling Out Your College Applications 11

When admissions officers are sitting around a table deciding who will be admitted, you won't be there to plead your case. You won't be able to explain how successful the club that you started to prevent students from dropping out of high school was or that you just missed winning the state golf title. The only thing at the table to tell the admissions officers about you is your application. It has to be filled out in such a way that the admissions officers can clearly see why you are so special that you should be admitted to their college.

Because your application can play an important part in the selection process, especially at selective schools, you want it to do an effective job of stating your strengths. As part of the application, you want to write an essay that expands your candidacy and choose teachers who will give you good recommendations. In this chapter, you will learn how to fill out college applications, write an essay, and get recommendations from your teachers so that your application gives the message "admit me" to admissions officers.

Getting an Application

As soon as you make your final decision on the colleges to which you will apply, make sure that you have admissions applications for these schools. You probably will have applications for many of them because schools often include applications with informational materials. If you need an application, write to the admissions office and request one using a letter similar to the one asking for information in chapter 10. Be sure you have or get a financial aid form if you will need help in financing your college education.

Hopefully, most of the schools will have applications available by the summer after your junior year so you can start filling them out before your busy senior year starts. When you receive an application, make several copies of it so you can practice filling out the copies before starting on the original form. The original should be put in a folder or envelope so it won't get wrinkled or torn. Place all the other forms and envelopes that you have to return to the college in the same folder or envelope. One caution: some applications have to be removed from books. Do this very carefully, as it is often quite easy to tear an edge.

Deciding Which Admissions Option Is Best

There is not just one application deadline at many colleges nor is there just one date on which all students will be notified if they have been admitted. Colleges have adopted a variety of admissions options because many students want to know early whether they have been accepted. If you have decided that one college is definitely your first choice, you may want to ask for an early admissions decision if this option is offered by the college. One of the first blanks to fill in on many applications is the box for the admissions option you want.

Regular admissions

The advantage of regular admissions is that it has the latest deadlines for applications to colleges. The disadvantage of this option is that it also has the latest notification dates for telling you whether you have been accepted. Selective schools will not usually send out this information until early April.

Most students choose to apply to college under the regular admission plan, which requires them to send in their applications by a certain date, usually in late fall or winter. Admissions decisions are then sent out to all candidates on the same date. Some colleges offer only the regular admissions option and do not have any early admissions plans.

Rolling admissions

Many colleges, especially large state universities, admit students on a continuing basis until the freshman class is full. As soon as your application is sent in, the admissions officers begin to process it. How soon you receive notification of admission depends on the school. It could be just a few weeks after you send in your application. Students whose grades and test scores are very close to minimum entrance requirements may have to wait quite a while for a decision. Because students are accepted on a first-come, first-served basis, it is to your advantage to apply early to these schools before the class is filled.

Early decision

If you have a strong high school record and really want to attend your first-choice college, you should consider applying for early decision. Usually, you apply in November and receive the school's decision in December. At that time, you are either accepted or rejected, or action on your application is deferred to the regular admissions deadline.

Each school that offers this admissions option has different rules, so you must be sure that you understand what is involved. By signing up for early admission, you agree to attend this college if you are accepted. Some schools let students apply to other schools at the same time; however, they must withdraw all other applications if accepted under early decision.

Early action

A few selective schools offer early action, which is similar to early decision. The main difference is that if you are accepted, you have until the regular admissions deadline to decide whether you want to attend that college. The students applying for this plan are usually very strong candidates.

Early evaluation

This plan is for the curious student who would like to know early what his or her chances for admission to a particular college are. Applications for early evaluation have to be submitted before applications for regular admissions. Then students learn between January and March whether their chances for admission are good, poor, or possible.

Decisions on admissions options

Look over the admissions options for each of the colleges where you are applying for admission. Decide which option you will use for each school. Be sure to study the rules for the early decision option carefully because some schools will not allow you to apply to other colleges if you select this option. Use the following chart to write down the admissions options you have chosen.

Admissions Options Chart					
Admissions Options	Names of Colleges				
Regular					
Rolling					
Early Decision					
Early Action					
Early Evaluation					

Keeping Track of Admissions Deadlines

If you are applying to several colleges, you will find it mind-boggling to keep track of all the different deadlines.

It is very difficult to do because the individual colleges will have different deadlines for when applications, financial aid, high school record, test scores, and teacher recommendation forms are due. Use the following chart to make sure you meet all these deadlines. As soon as you get an application, enter all the deadlines on this chart. Then draw a line through each deadline as you meet it.

Your Applications Checklist Deadlines					
Deadlines for Applications	Names of Colleges				
Financial aid application					
Teacher reference forms					
High school record form					
ACT or SAT results reaching school					
Results for Achievement Tests reaching school					
First semester report form					
Sending additional information					

Guidelines for Filling Out Your Applications

Fill your applications out early and mail them well before the deadlines. This gives the admissions officers a chance to study your application rather than speed-read it along with all the other applications that were submitted at the last minute. Here are some basic steps that you should follow in filling out your applications:

Read the entire application. Always read the entire application through several times so you clearly understand what information is required in each section.

Read the directions carefully. Never put a mark on an application before you have read the directions. Then follow them to the letter.

Practice on the copy. Fill out your complete application on the copy before filling out the original. This way you will know how to space what you want to say.

Be very neat. Try to type your application or use an erasable pen and your best handwriting.

Use the space wisely. Stay within the space allotted for your answers. The space indicates how much information the colleges want. If you absolutely must have more space to answer a question, attach an additional sheet of paper rather than try to cram your answer into a small space.

Be truthful. You are describing the real you and your actual accomplishments. You want this to agree with what the school record and your recommendations say. It is not necessary, however, to point out your weaknesses.

Pay attention to details. Don't forget to answer any questions. Remember to sign your application.

Proofread your application. Never mail an application until you have carefully proofread it. Watch for spelling and grammar errors.

Photocopy your completed application. This is simple insurance in case it gets misplaced in your home, the mail, or the admissions office.

Filling Out an Actual Application

Some college applications are a breeze to fill out—no more than a page of general information is required. The more selective the admissions process is at a school, the greater the amount of information you will have to provide. You will also have to write short answers and longer essays. To help you understand how to fill out an application, fill out the actual application provided on the next four pages. This application is called the Common Application, and it can be used in place of the individual applications of over 100 colleges. You fill out this application and then have it photocopied for each listed college to which you are applying. Using the Common Application is a timesaver for students.

You can obtain a Common Application from your high school guidance or career office or by writing to the National Association of Secondary School Principals, 1904 Association Drive, Reston, Virginia 22091. Once you have filled out this application, you will find it much easier to fill out other applications, also.

Looking at the Common Application

When you look at the Common Application, you will see at the top of the first page the list of colleges using this application. Study the list carefully, as one or more of the schools on your final list might use this application. Some of the colleges using this application will want additional supplementary material which they will tell you about as soon as your application is received at the college.

Read through the entire application to get a feel for what type of information you need to provide. The Common Application, like other applications, is broken down into several sections requiring different types of information. You are asked to provide:

personal data

extracurricular and personal activities

educational data

work experience

test information

personal statement (essay)

academic honors

Agnes Scott ● Alfred ● Allegheny ● American University ● Antioch ● Bard ● Bates ● Beloit ● Bennington ● Boston University ● Brandeis
Bryn Mawr ● Bucknell ● Carleton ● Case Western Reserve ● Centenary College ● Centre ● Claremont McKenna ● Clark University ● Coe ● Colby-Sawyer
Colgate ● Colorado College ● Denison ● University of Denver ● DePauw ● Dickinson ● Drew ● Earlham ● Eckerd ● Elmira ● Emory ● Fairfield ● Fisk
Fordham ● Franklin & Marshall ● Gettysburg ● Goucher ● Grinnell ● Guilford ● Hamilton ● Hampden-Sydney ● Hampshire ● Hartwick ● Haverford
Hobart ● Hood ● Kalamazoo ● Kenyon   Knox ● Lafayette ● Lawrence ● Lehigh
Lewis and Clark ● Linfield ● Macalester   Manhattan ● Manhattanville ● Mills
Millsaps ● Morehouse ● Mount Holyoke   **COMMON APPLICATION**   Muhlenberg ● New York University ● Oberlin
Occidental ● Ohio Wesleyan ● Pitzer   Pomona ● University of Puget Sound
Randolph-Macon ● Randolph-Macon Woman's   University of Redlands ● Reed College
Rensselaer Polytechnic ● Rhodes ● Rice ● University of Richmond ● Ripon ● University of Rochester ● Rollins ● St. Lawrence ● St. Olaf
Salem ● Sarah Lawrence ● Scripps ● Simmons ● Skidmore ● Smith ● University of the South ● University of Southern California
Southern Methodist ● Spelman ● Stetson ● Susquehanna ● Swarthmore ● Texas Christian ● Trinity College ● Trinity University
Tulane ● Union ● Valparaiso ● Vanderbilt ● Vassar ● Wake Forest ● Washington College ● Washington and Lee ● Wells ● Wesleyan
Western Maryland ● Wheaton ● Whitman ● Willamette ● William Smith ● Williams ● Wooster ● Worcester Polytechnic

APPLICATION FOR UNDERGRADUATE ADMISSION

The colleges and universities listed above encourage the use of this application. No distinction will be made between it and the college's own form. The accompanying instructions tell you how to complete, copy, and file your application to any one or several of the colleges. Please type or print in black ink.

PERSONAL DATA

Legal name: _____   _____
             Last   *First*   *Middle (complete)*   *Jr., etc.*   *Sex*

Prefer to be called: _____(nickname)   Former last name(s) if any: _____

Are you applying as a ☐ freshman or ☐ transfer student?   For the term beginning: _____

Permanent home address: _____
                                               Number and Street

_____
          City or Town   *County*   *State*   *Zip*

If different from the above, please give your mailing address for all admission correspondence:

Mailing address: _____
                                               Number and Street

_____
          City or Town   *State*   *Zip*

Telephone at mailing address: _____ / _____ Permanent home telephone: _____ / _____
                              Area Code   *Number*   *Area Code*   *Number*
Birthdate: _____ Citizenship: ☐ U.S. ☐ Permanent Resident U.S. ☐ Other _____ Visa type _____
          Month Day Year   *Country*

Possible area(s) of academic concentration/major: _____ or undecided ☐

Special college or division if applicable: _____

Possible career or professional plans: _____ or undecided ☐

Will you be a candidate for financial aid?   Yes _____   No _____   If yes, the appropriate form(s) was/will

be filed on: _____

The following items are optional:

Social Security number, if any: ☐ ☐ ☐ ☐ ☐ ☐ ☐ ☐ ☐

Place of birth: _____ Marital status: _____ Height: _____ Weight: _____
                City   *State*   *Country*
Parents' country of birth: Mother _____ Father _____

What is your first language, if other than English? _____

How would you describe yourself: (Please check one)
   ☐ American Indian or Alaskan Native   ☐ Hispanic (including Puerto Rican)
   ☐ Asian or Pacific Islander (including Indian subcontinent)   ☐ White, Anglo, Caucasian (non-Hispanic)
   ☐ Black (non-Hispanic)   ☐ Other (Specify)

EDUCATIONAL DATA

School you attend now _____ ACT/CEEB code number _____

Address _____
                        City   *State*   *Zip Code*
Date of secondary graduation _____ Is your school public? _____ private? _____ parochial? _____

College advisor: _____ School telephone: _____ / _____
                        Name   *Position*   *Area Code*   *Number*   **APP**

List all other secondary schools, including summer schools and programs you have attended beginning with ninth grade.

Name of School	Location (City, State, Zip)	Dates Attended

List all colleges at which you have taken courses for credit and list names of courses on a separate sheet. Please have a transcript sent from each institution as soon as possible.

Name of College	Location (City, State, Zip)	Degree Candidate?	Dates Attended

If not currently attending school, please check here: ☐ Describe in detail, on a separate sheet, your activities since last enrolled.

TEST INFORMATION. Be sure to note the tests required for each institution to which you are applying. The official scores from the appropriate testing agency must be submitted to each institution as soon as possible. Please list your test plans below.

	Scholastic Aptitude Test (SAT)	Achievement Tests (ACH)	Subject	American College Test (ACT)
Dates taken or				
to be taken				

FAMILY

Mother's full name: _____ Is she living? _____

Home address if different from yours: _____

Occupation: _____
(Describe briefly)   *(Name of business or organization)*

Name of college (if any): _____ Degree: _____ Year: _____

Name of professional or graduate school (if any): _____ Degree: _____ Year: _____

Father's full name: _____ Is he living? _____

Home address if different from yours: _____

Occupation: _____
(Describe briefly)   *(Name of business or organization)*

Name of college (if any): _____ Degree: _____ Year: _____

Name of professional or graduate school (if any): _____ Degree: _____ Year: _____

If not with both parents, with whom do you make your permanent home: _____

Please check if parents are ☐ separated   ☐ divorced

Please give names and ages of your brothers or sisters. If they have attended college, give the names of the institutions attended, degrees, and approximate dates:

ACADEMIC HONORS

Briefly describe any scholastic distinctions or honors you have won beginning with ninth grade:

_____

_____

_____

EXTRACURRICULAR AND PERSONAL ACTIVITIES

Please list your principal extracurricular, community, and family activities and hobbies in the order of their interest to you. Include specific events and/or major accomplishments such as musical instrument played, varsity letters earned, etc. Please (✔) in the right column those activities you hope to pursue in college.

Activity	Grade level or post-secondary (p.s.)					Approximate time spent		Positions held, honors won, or letters earned	Do you plan to participate in college?
	9	10	11	12	P.S.	Hours per week	Weeks per year		

WORK EXPERIENCE

List any job (including summer employment) you have held during the past three years.

Specific nature of work	Employer	Approximate dates of employment	Approximate no. of hours spent per week

In the space provided below, briefly discuss which of these activities (extracurricular and personal activities or work experience) has had the most meaning for you, and why.

_____

_____

_____

_____

_____

PERSONAL STATEMENT

This personal statement helps us become acquainted with you in ways different from courses, grades, test scores, and other objective data. *It enables you to demonstrate your ability to organize thoughts and express yourself. Please write an essay about one of the topics listed below.* You may attach extra pages (same size, please) if your essay exceeds the limits of this page.

1) Evaluate a significant experience or achievement that has special meaning to you.
2) Discuss some issue of personal, local, or national concern and its importance to you.
3) Indicate a person who has had a significant influence on you, and describe that influence.

I understand that: (1) it is my responsibility to report any changes in my schedule to the colleges to which I am applying, and (2) *if I am an Early Decision Candidate, that I must attach a letter with this application notifying that college of my intent.*

My signature below indicates that all information contained in my application is complete, factually correct, and honestly presented.

Signature _____ Date _____

These colleges are committed to administer all educational policies and activities without discrimination on the basis of race, color, religion, national or ethnic origin, age, handicap, or sex. The admissions process at private undergraduate institutions is exempt from the federal regulation implementing Title IX of the Education Amendments of 1972.

You will notice at once that the written record you made in chapter 8 of all the things that you have done in high school will make it very easy for you to fill out the information sections of the application. However, before you begin to fill out the application, think carefully of the image you wish to present to the admissions officers. Is it as a serious student; an accomplished artist, musician, actor, or writer; an athlete; or an all-around student? Since you can't use every detail in your written record, use the ones that support how you want the admissions officers to see you.

Completing the personal data section

The first part of this section is largely devoted to facts that will help the school identify you. Remember to use the same name as you did for registering for the admissions tests. If you use a nickname instead of a first name, be sure to write it down. This is the name that you want to find on the door to your room and in the freshman photo book when you arrive on campus. There isn't really space to write out your birthdate, so use numbers. If you check the box for U.S. citizenship, you don't need to write any more on that line.

Possible major. Before you fill in your choice of major, be sure that you can answer "yes" to these questions:

1. Does the college offer that major? (Many schools do not have prelaw, premedicine, or business majors. Check the catalog.)   yes   no

2. Did I demonstrate strength in this area in high school? (In other words, don't choose French as a major if you have all C grades.)   yes   no

3. Does the choice of a certain major affect my admission chances at a state school? (Some majors, like computer science, are very popular so admission with this major can be more competitive.)   yes   no

Special college or division. Most students will leave this line blank. But look in a catalog if you are interested in a field like mining, art, nursing, agriculture, engineering, or music to see if there are special colleges or divisions for these fields within a school.

Possible career plans. College admissions officers do not really expect you to know what you will be doing in four years, so an "undecided" answer is perfectly acceptable here. Also, for possible major don't choose a career that is incompatible with your high school grades and interests.

Financial aid. You will learn all about financial aid in chapter 12. Check "yes" if you need financial aid. Most colleges do not consider financial need in making admissions decisions. Find out the financial aid deadlines so you will file your form on time.

Optional items. There is no reason not to fill in this section. If you are a member of a minority, it may be decidedly to your advantage to describe yourself, as schools actively seek minority applicants.

Completing the educational data section

On the Common Application as well as most other applications, this is a very simple section to complete. The ACT-/CEEB code number is the same number you used in registering for college entrance tests. Your college advisor is usually your guidance counselor unless a different person handles this task at your school. Do fill in all the blanks in this section as a college may need to contact your school for more information about you.

Completing the test information section

Note in this section you are being asked only when you have taken or will take the SAT, Achievement Tests, or ACT. On some applications you will be asked for test scores. When writing down the test dates, it is sufficient to list just the month and year.

Completing the family section

The family information section lets colleges know what your family background is. It also does one other thing: it lets the colleges know where members of your family went to college. If you parents, brothers, or sisters happened to attend a college to which you are applying, this will give you an admissions advantage. The more selective the college, the more important the alumni connection is in the admissions process.

Listing your academic honors

Here is one section where reading directions counts. Note you are being asked to list only *academic* honors, not other honors like prom queen or most valuable player. And you are also being asked to start your list with honors won beginning in the ninth grade, so do put your honors in the correct chronological order. Since the space is limited, go back to chapter 8 and choose only the most important academic honors from your listing of honors, awards, and prizes. If you have won the same honor more than once, list the honor followed by the years it was won, for example, Top 25—9, 10, 11.

Listing extracurricular and personal activities

One of the important factors that colleges consider in deciding whether to admit students is their participation in extracurricular activities. So fill this section in carefully, being sure to select your most significant accomplishments outside of the classroom. Look at the list of extracurricular activities that you made in chapter 8 in order to complete this section. Also notice that the colleges want to hear about family activities and hobbies that interest you. So here is the place to mention you are a gourmet cook, needlepoint expert, computer programmer, or skilled car mechanic. It is also the spot to list travel experiences and lessons that you have taken in a variety of things from ice skating to cello. Again, it is important to read and follow the directions. You are to list the activities in the order of their interest to you.

Because the space is limited, you should realize that the colleges don't want a long list of activities that are not really important to you. This is also obvious because they are asking how much time you devote to each activity in a week. You won't need to list any club that meets only once or twice in a semester, but you will certainly want to list any club in which you hold an office or are actively involved in some way or a sport that requires some of your time each week. Students who don't find the space sufficient for listing all of their activities should type or write at the bottom of this chart, "See additional listings on attached page." They can then complete their listings on the extra page, which should also have their name and address on it.

When filling out this list, you want to make sure that you give specific rather than general information for the activity column. Don't use a broad term like *music*. Instead, use narrower terms like *pep band* or *concert orchestra*. Make sure what you write in the "positions held, honors won, or letters earned" column clearly reflects the part you have played in an activity. This is not an easy task in the limited space provided; however, using abbreviations like MVP for most valuable player can help. Also, you can use two lines for an activity, if appropriate. See how much information the following entries for this column give:

Extracurricular and Personal Activities

Please list your principal extracurricular, community, and family activities and hobbies in the order of their interest to you. Include specific events and/or major accomplishments such as musical instrument played, varsity letters earned, etc. Please (ν) in the right column those activities you hope to pursue in college.

Activity	Grade level or post-secondary (p.s.) 9 10 11 12 P.S.					Approximate time spent Hours per week	Weeks per year	Positions held, honors won, or letters earned	Do you plan to participate in college?
Varsity Tennis	x	x	x	x		14	50	Cpt., MVP—12 State Dbls. Chmp.—9	x
Student Council		x		x		1	36	President—12	x
Inner-city Big Brother			x	x		2	50	Tutor a fifth grader	x
Newspaper	x	x				5	36	10—Sports Editor 9—Copy Editor	
TV-Brain Game Team			x	x		?		11—State Runner-up	
Electric guitar	x	x	x	x		3	40	9–12—Rock Band	

Don't worry about explaining your activities as fully as you want in this section. In the section at the bottom of the page, you have an opportunity to discuss either an activity or work experience that has had the most meaning for you in greater detail.

Completing the work experience section

Besides grades, test scores, and extracurricular activities, colleges also consider your work experience when making admissions decisions. You may not have held a steady job, but colleges want to hear about temporary jobs like baby-sitting and yard work. Begin this section with your most recent job. If you need additional space to relate all the jobs that you have held, attach an extra page or put this information on the extra page for activities. Be sure to be specific in describing your jobs.

Writing about your activities

When you write on the Common Application about the activity or work experience that has had the most meaning for you, your application becomes more than a basic information sheet. You are letting the admissions officers know why you use your time in a particular way. Consider this brief discussion or any questions that you are asked to answer on an application as a mini essay. Write with care just like you will on essays. Do stay within the allotted space, as the colleges are asking for a short answer.

Writing the personal statement or essay

If you write the most fabulous essay that grips the imagination of every admissions officer at a college, will it improve your chances of admission? Yes. Writing a poor essay with spelling and grammar errors can also hurt your chances. When colleges ask for you to write an essay or personal statement as the Common Application does, the essay does play a part in the admissions process, but it certainly isn't the major factor in determining whether or not you will be admitted.

The point of the college application essay, according to Paul Thiboutot, Dean of Admissions at Carleton College, is to help the admissions officers gain some insight into the personal aspect of the candidate—how the candidate thinks and uses his or her time. Essays should also show substance and good writing. So use the essay or essays you write to expand your candidacy beyond grades, test scores, and lists of accomplishments to show the person you are.

Also use your essay or essays to establish yourself as a good writer capable of clearly expressing your thoughts while using correct grammar and spelling. In other words, write an essay that would receive an A in your English class.

Guidelines for writing an essay

Whether an essay is assigned or you have to choose a topic, there are certain guidelines that you must follow.

Write it yourself. Ask your English teacher, friends, or parents to make suggestions, but don't let them rewrite your paper because it won't sound like you.

Give yourself time. Start early enough so you have sufficient time to write, rewrite, and proofread all of your essays.

Stick to the topic. Colleges want to see how all their applicants discuss a stated topic or answer the same question.

Be organized. Follow the same steps that you do in writing essays for your classes. Have an introduction, body, and conclusion to your essay.

Use your own language. Admissions officers are not impressed by fancy words taken from a thesaurus.

Add dimension to your application. Don't repeat what you have already said in the information sections of your application.

Keep your essays brief. Stay within the space limit. Extra pages do not impress admissions officers.

Be careful with humor. Humor can add life to your essay. Make sure it also reveals you as a clever, not a shallow, person.

Be original. Don't quote well-known phrases that thousands of applicants have used before you. Forget about what Robert Frost, Martin Luther King, and William Shakespeare have said.

Be specific. Every year applicants write about such generalities as wanting world peace, obtaining a liberal arts education, and expanding their horizons. Narrow your focus to specifics like the feelings of a Vietnamese refugee, learning to appreciate poetry, and studying in Spain.

Proofread. Check once, twice, three times that what you have written is correct. Have others proofread your essays, too.

Adapt essays for reuse. One essay cannot possibly be used on all applications because few questions and essay topics are identical.

Always write optional essays. This is just one more chance to let admissions officers learn more about you and set you apart from other candidates.

Evaluating an essay

Carefully read the following essay, which was written to discuss the second topic on the personal statement about some issue of personal, local, or national concern and its importance to you. Then use the following chart to evaluate it.

A significant problem facing my generation is the aging of the United States population. Today there are nearly ten times as many people over sixty-five as there were in 1900. Never before has the possibility existed of a society having as many older people as young people. This is the condition forecast for the United States in 2030 when my generation reaches sixty-five.

Long before my generation reaches sixty-five, we will have to face some of the problems of an aging population. The cost of providing a long and comfortable retirement for so many people has already created serious financial problems in the social security system. All programs for older Americans now constitute approximately 25 percent of the federal budget. The elderly's share of the budget could soar to over 60 percent by 2030 if the current programs remain unchanged. This would cause financial problems of disastrous proportions. Even though a large amount of money is now being spent on older people, almost one-third of the elderly live in poverty or near poverty.

The problems of an aging population are not limited to the financial sphere. Older people have more health problems than younger people. More hospitals, nursing homes, and medical personnel will be required as the population continues to grow older. The percentage of people in the work force will decline as the population ages. A shortage of workers may occur.

Not only must my generation solve some of these significant problems of an aging population, we must also find a useful role for older people in the United States in order to make our own futures bright. As individuals we can begin by finding ways to improve the relationships between young and old in our own families. As a group we can work for the implementation of policies that encourage a longer worklife and a shorter retirement.

Grading the essay. Give the essay a grade from A to F in each of the following areas. Then give it an overall grade.

Organization ____ Originality ____ Narrow Focus ____

Grammar ____ Language ____

Overall Grade ____

Writing your own essay

Use the space on the application to write your own essay on one of the three topics. When you are finished writing the essay, proofread it using the questions in chapter 5. Then give your essay a grade using the following criteria. The sample essay would have received a C from an admissions officer at a selective school.

Organization ___ Originality ___ Narrow Focus ___

Grammar ___ Language ___

Overall Grade ___

Getting the Recommendations You Need

When you fill out a college application, you are telling your story about what you have done in high school. When teachers write recommendations for you, they are reinforcing what you have said plus telling about how they think you will handle college. Recommendations can both improve and hurt your chances for admission, so it is very important to choose teachers who will write the best recommendations for you.

What teachers will be asked about you

To help colleges make admissions decisions, teachers are asked to rate or describe your academic performance, intellectual promise, and personal qualities. Many colleges use a checklist similar to the one in chapter 3. Others may ask questions like the following ones:

- What can you tell us about the applicant's intellectual qualities and academic work?

- What are the first words that come to your mind to describe this applicant's character?

- What is the quality of the applicant's performance in extracurricular, community, or work activities?

- How do you think this applicant would do on personal and academic grounds at this college?

On almost all recommendation forms teachers are asked how long they have known applicants as well as what subjects they have taught the applicant. They may also be asked what grades they have given the applicant. In choosing a teacher to write recommendations, you should consider how the teacher would answer the preceding questions.

Selecting teachers to write recommendations

Obviously you want to select teachers who will write positive, if not glowing, recommendations about you. The teacher should usually be one who has taught you recently in an academic class. It is also a good idea to choose teachers from different areas if you are asked to submit more than one recommendation. If you have listed a major, it makes sense to choose a teacher in that area as one of your recommenders.

Write down on the following chart the names of at least four teachers you may want to have write recommendations for you. Now answer the following questions about each teacher with a "yes" or "no."

Evaluating Recommenders					
Question	Names of Teachers				
1. Is the teacher a good writer? (English teachers usually are.)					
2. Have you had a class from this teacher recently? (It's been a long time since you studied freshman biology.)					
3. Does this teacher really know you?					
4. Has this teacher worked as a sponsor or coach of one of your extracurricular activities?					
5. Does this teacher like you?					
6. Will this teacher write a strong recommendation for you? (If uncertain, ask the teacher.)					
7. Will this teacher complete and mail the recommendation on time?					
8. Did this teacher attend the college that you want to attend? (It helps if the teacher knows the school.)					
Total number of "yes" answers:					

Choose the teachers who had the most "yes" answers to write your recommendations. You may be surprised to learn that your favorite teachers are not the ones you chose. Because it takes time to write recommendations, you may want to ask more than one or two teachers to do this for you. If you are convinced that one teacher is the best choice, you might suggest that the teacher write a recommendation on school stationery and make copies of it.

Help your teachers write
your recommendations

The earlier in your senior year you ask teachers to write recommendations for you, the fewer the number of forms they will be busy completing for other students. Once a teacher has agreed to write a recommendation, ask for a conference to talk about your college plans. Take to this meeting recommendation forms and stamped, addressed envelopes. You also should hand the teacher a letter giving deadline dates for each recommendation and a description of what you have been doing in high school. This background information will help the teacher remember your achievements when writing the recommendation. Complete the following exercise so you will know what to say in your letter.

Dear _____

    I enjoy(ed) being in your _____

course(s) because _____

_____

_____.

    To assist you in completing my recommendation

form(s), I want to tell you about some of my activities dur-

ing high school. My favorite extracurricular activity has

been _____.

Participation in this activity has included doing such

things as _____

_____

_____

_____.

I have also participated in these activities: _____

_____

_____.

Outside of school my principal interests have been _____

_____

_____

_____ .

The college deadline(s) for receiving these recommendations is (are):

(college)   (deadline)

_____   _____

_____   _____

I appreciate your help in writing this (these) recommendations for me.

Sincerely,

_____

Waiving your rights. On most recommendation forms, there is a box asking if you want to waive your rights to see the teacher's recommendation provided you enroll in that college. It is best to waive this right because the admissions officers then know that the teacher is free to write a recommendation that you will not be reading. Sign this waiver before giving the recommendation form to a teacher.

Evaluation by college advisor or guidance counselor

Besides giving recommendation forms to teachers, you will need to give a school report form to your college advisor, who usually is your guidance counselor. This form asks about your class rank and often asks the counselor to rate certain characteristics on a checklist and to answer questions similar to those on the teacher recommendation forms. Because the counselor is rating you, it is to your advantage to have shared your college plans with him or her. It is also a good idea to check over your transcript with the counselor to make sure it is accurate in every way, as this is the record of your grades and activities that will be sent to the colleges. Be sure to thank your counselor for completing the school report form in a letter. You may also want to include in the letter the same background information that you gave to the teachers writing recommendations for you.

Should you send extra recommendations?

Colleges will usually ask you to submit one, two, or three recommendations. There is no reason to submit extra recommendations unless they will add dimension to your application. It is a good idea to submit a recommendation from a coach or an art, music, or other special subjects teacher if you have special talents in those areas that you want to pursue at college. Most colleges are looking for applicants who are exceptional in one area. This could give you an edge in the admissions process. For the same reason, you may also want to talk to college coaches, music conductors, and others since they can put in a good word for you at the admissions office. You can also submit a recommendation from a boss or someone with whom you have worked as a volunteer. Recommendations from political leaders and prominent alumni have no value unless these people know you well.

Supporting Your Application

You have probably heard about students sending such intriguing items as newspaper articles about themselves, fabulous desserts for the admissions officers, and original operas along with their applications. Extra materials can help students be admitted if they really add something to the student's application by showing a skill or talent not documented thoroughly. One caution—make sure that a college wants to receive extra materials. Some colleges will even tell you how to submit them. Be careful about submitting gimmicks like T-shirts and cartoons, as the admissions officers may not find them clever. Look over this list of materials that are often sent to colleges and decide if any of them might enhance your application:

- photographs of art works
- artwork—sculpture, paintings, pottery, jewelry
- photographs—if you are an amateur photographer
- tapes of solo musical performances
- tapes of original musical compositions
- newspaper stories written by applicant
- newspaper stories of an *outstanding*, not routine, accomplishment
- samples of excellent poetry or short stories
- published materials
- computer programs
- videos of sports, musical, or theatrical performances

Updating your application

If you send your application in early, exciting things like winning first place in debating in your state, getting the lead in the senior play, or having a children's book published can happen. Since any one of these or similar things could improve your chances of admission, you want colleges where you are applying to know about them. Some schools provide a form that you can use to send new information. Or you can send the information on a sheet of paper that also tells when you are applying for admission and gives your name, address, and social security number.

The Final Steps

Reread your application immediately after completing it. Then put it aside and read it again the next day to make a final check for errors. Finally, copy your application and mail it. If the college will not be sending you a postcard saying that the application has been received, have the post office send a return receipt request along with the application so you know that it reached the college.

Finding Out about Financial Aid

12

You have probably heard that billions of dollars of financial aid are available for college students each year. This is certainly true. But did you also know that students and their parents have the major responsibility for paying for college even though many students receive financial aid?

Colleges don't just give out financial aid. It is your job to find out what aid is available and to apply for it. This requires considerable research. Besides reading this chapter, you are going to have to talk to your parents, your high school counselor, and college financial aid officers. You will also find it helpful to read books like the following ones:

Don't Miss Out, Robert Leider and Anna Leider, Octameron Press. This book will tell you just about everything you need to know about financial aid.

The Public Ivies, Richard Moll, Viking Penguin, Inc.

The author reveals how to get an ivy league education at state-supported schools.

How the Military Will Help You Pay for College, Don M. Betterton, Peterson's Guides, Inc. You will find out about hundreds of different military college aid funds by reading this book.

In this chapter, you will find out more about what college will cost, the types of aid that are available, and how to go about obtaining financial aid. This chapter will get you started in the search for the financial aid you need.

What Will Your College Education Cost?

How much your education costs obviously depends on where you go to college. The difference in cost between going to a community college and an ivy league school is enormous. However, you don't want to rule out applying to a school just because of its cost. If you qualify for financial aid, you could find it no more expensive to go to Harvard or Princeton than to attend a state-supported school.

In chapter 10, you made a rough estimate of what several colleges you were considering would cost based only on tuition and room and board. To get a more accurate picture of costs at individual colleges, you need to add such expenses as books and supplies, fees, transportation, and personal expenses. You can get information about the cost of these items from college directories or directly from the financial aid offices of colleges.

Because personal expenses vary considerably from student to student, you should figure what your current personal expenses are rather than using a college's estimate for an average student. This will give you a more realistic budget. Use the following chart to compute your current monthly expenditures. Then multiply by the number of months you will be in school to get your personal expenses for a year in college.

clothing _____

personal care (toiletries) _____

telephone (remember long distance) _____

entertainment _____

records and tapes _____

snacks　　　　　　　　　　　　　　　　　_____

restaurants　　　　　　　　　　　　　　_____

automobile (if applicable)　　　　　　_____

laundry and cleaners　　　　　　　　_____

other　　　　　　　　　　　　　　　　　_____

Total monthly expenses　　　　　　$_____

Total yearly expenses　　　　　　　$_____

Estimated college costs. Fill in the following chart to establish what your costs will be at the colleges where you are applying for admission.

	Names of Colleges				
Estimated Costs					
Tuition and fees					
Housing					
Meals					
Books and supplies					
Transportation (to and from school)					
Personal expenses					
Total Estimated Cost					

Determination of financial need. It is important to know whether you will need financial aid at the colleges where you will be applying. Use the following chart to determine your financial need at each of these schools. This amount is almost always greater than what the government or colleges believe you will need to attend college.

	Names of Colleges				
Financial Need Factors					
Estimated cost of college					
Student contribution					
Summer savings					
Family contribution					
Financial need					

Where the Money Comes From

Most of the money students receive for financial aid comes from the federal government, state governments, and the college's own resources and private sources, with the lion's share of aid coming from the federal government. Some colleges have a lot more money available for financial aid than others. The basic types of aid which students receive are grants, loans, and employment. You may receive just one type of aid or some combination of the three types of financial aid.

Grants do not have to be repaid

For students, grants are the best possible source of financial aid, as they do not have to be repaid. The federal government, state governments, and colleges have grant programs. Most grants are awarded on the basis of need. Scholarships can also be included in this category even though they are often based on achievement as well as need. Scholarships can be obtained from an amazing number of sources.

Although there are many grants and scholarships available, the federal government provides the most financial aid in this category through Pell Grants and Supplementary Education Opportunity Grants (SEOG).

Pell Grants. All students who are applying for financial aid should apply for a Pell Grant because schools do not usually put together financial aid packages for applicants until they know whether or not the applicants are eligible for Pell Grants. By legislation, this grant is available only to undergraduates who meet a certain standard of need. The amount of money available for Pell Grants varies, as Congress determines the funding each year. If you meet the need requirement for this grant, you will receive aid.

Supplementary Education Opportunity Grants. This government grant program, which is administered by colleges, is for those students with the greatest financial need. Since each college receives only a certain amount of money for these grants, it is a good idea to apply early before the money runs out. Pell Grant recipients are given priority in receiving this grant.

State programs. Every state has its own grant and scholarship programs. The programs are based on both need and scholastic achievement. There are also some programs for students who want to pursue a career in a certain area like teaching or health care as well as programs for the children of veterans. In some cases, it is necessary to take competitive examinations to get this aid. Students usually have to be residents of the state and attend college within the state to get financial aid from a state program. You can find out about these programs from your counselor or the state's higher education agency.

College programs. Colleges have their own resources that allow them to provide scholarships and grants. You will have to check each college to find out what is available.

Loans have to be repaid

While loans help you get an education, they can also mean you are facing a tremendous debt burden in the future. When you graduate or leave school, you have to start repaying your college loans. On certain loans you even have to start paying interest while you are in school. Some loans are reduced if you join the military or do some type of public service. Repayment may also be delayed if you go to graduate school or serve in the military, Peace Corps, or

Vista. Loans like the following ones play a big part in most students' financial aid packages.

Stafford Student Loans. This is the major loan program at most colleges. To be eligible for this loan you must apply for a Pell Grant and show financial need. There are limits on the amount of money that can be borrowed each year as well as a limit on the total amount that can be borrowed as an undergraduate. You obtain this loan from a bank or other lending agency, but it is guaranteed by the federal government. The advantages of this loan are that you do not pay interest while you are attending school and repayment is at a government subsidized rate.

Perkins Loans. The federal government provides the money for these loans, and the colleges act as the lenders. There are limits to the amount of money that can be borrowed.

Parent Loans to Undergraduate Students (PLUS). These loans, which are guaranteed by the federal government, are taken out by parents—not students. It is not necessary to show financial need to get one of these loans. These loans are made by a variety of lending agencies and repayment starts sixty days after the money is received. Colleges have applications for these loans.

State loans. State governments also offer a wide variety of loan programs.

College loans. Colleges offer loans to students from their own resources.

Private loans. Many lending agencies, employers, and organizations offer low-interest educational loans.

Employment is helping yourself

Many students work to pay for part of their education. Colleges administer work-study programs with money that is largely received from the federal government, although some state governments also have work-study programs.

These jobs are usually on the college campus, but they can also be with nonprofit organizations. Students work from 10 to 20 hours a week for at least minimum wage. Jobs can range from being a food handler to a research assistant. Eligibility for work-study programs is based on need and availability of funds. Besides the government work-study programs, many colleges also have their own employment programs.

Steps to Getting Financial Aid

Because applying for financial aid can be quite confusing, you begin this process by talking to your guidance counselor or college advisor at your high school. These people know what financial aid programs are available and how to apply for them. All college financial aid offices also have counselors who are willing to talk to you in the office or answer questions on the phone. Whenever you have questions from how to fill out forms to where to find aid, talk to people in your high school guidance or career office or in the financial aid office of a college. You need their expert advice. Don't try to do this by yourself.

The first step—applying for government and college aid

Since most financial aid money comes from the government and colleges, it only makes sense to apply for that money first. You begin by filing a need analysis form. It will probably be the Financial Aid Form (FAF) of the College Scholarship Service of the College Board for colleges that use the SAT. Colleges that use the ACT will want you to use the Family Financial Statement (FFS) of the American College Testing Program. A few states have their own need analysis forms. You can get these forms at your high school guidance or career office or the financial aid office of a college. When you fill in one of these forms you are applying for the following financial aid programs:

- federal student financial aid programs

- state scholarship and grant programs

- college programs where you are applying for admission

You can't send need analysis forms in before January 1 of the year you are applying to college, but you want to get the forms after they come out in November or December and send them in as close to January 1 as possible because some aid is dispensed on a first-come, first-served basis.

It takes about three hours to fill in one of these forms. You give information about the size of your family, debt, education expenses, and unusual expenses as well as your own and your family's incomes and assets. Fill this form out very carefully, as any errors or omissions will only delay the processing of your application. Be sure to make copies of this form before mailing it with a return receipt requested to a need analysis service.

The need analysis services all use the same formula to determine the amount of money you and your family should contribute to your college education. Within approximately two to six weeks, you learn what a service estimates your family contribution should be and the same information in greater detail is sent to the colleges you have indicated on the need analysis form. The amount of money you and your family are expected to contribute will be the same at all colleges.

College financial aid applications. Besides filling out the need analysis form, you will have to submit an application for financial aid to many colleges where you are applying for admission. Fortunately, these forms are considerably easier to complete. Again, it is a good idea to submit these applications well before the deadlines, as colleges do run out of aid money. It is important for you to remember that colleges have a great number of financial aid programs that are funded with their own money.

The second step—looking for more financial aid

There is a lot of financial aid that is not supplied by government and college programs, but this aid is a lot harder to find. Start your search in your high school's guidance or career office to see what is available in your own community. Then check to see what is available at colleges where you are applying for admission. Finally, take the time to read through directories like the following in your high school or public library as they will have enormous lists of aid programs for which you can apply.

The College Blue Book: Scholarships, Fellowships, Grants and Loans

Chronicle Sports Guide: Intercollegiate Athletics and Scholarships
    Directory of Financial Aids for Minorities
    Financial Aids for Higher Education
    Student Aid Annual

Look at the following list of sources of financial aid and check those that might be a source of aid for you. Then investigate them locally and in directories.

____school clubs (4-H, Deca)

____parents' employment

____parents' union

____parents' clubs (civic, fraternal)

____academic scholarship (newspaper carrier, fast food worker, caddie)

____religious affiliation

____parents' military service

____sports scholarship

____special talent scholarship (art, music)

____professional organizations in career area (accounting, health, education, engineering)

____nationality

____minority

____handicapped

____the military

Putting together a financial aid package

Once the financial aid office receives the figures on your expected family contribution from a need analysis service plus a list of some of the other financial aid that you are eligible for, the office staff is ready to put together a financial aid package that meets your needs. You should be aware that some colleges using their own need formulas often increase the amount of money that families are expected to contribute.

No two colleges will develop the same financial aid package for you. The first money that goes into the package is money from Pell Grants and state programs. Then money is placed in the package from other federal programs and state and college programs plus any money that you have acquired from scholarships. You learn about your financial aid package in an award letter from each college. You have the option of rejecting part of this package. There are also deadlines for accepting the package.

How can you get more money?

Unfortunately, you don't find out what your expected family contribution will be until some time after January 1. And you don't find out what your financial aid package will be at a college until after January 1 and after you have been admitted to that school. By the time you have all this information, it is often too late to get more money. So you should explore the following options for getting more money early in your senior year if your own estimates indicate that you will need financial aid.

The military. You probably have heard of ROTC programs and the military academies; however, there are hundreds of other programs funded by the military. All of these programs require some military service.

Cooperative education. Under this program, which many colleges have, you combine your college studies with an off-campus job. The job will usually pay for the cost of your education.

Cost-cutters. Think of living at home and attending a local college for one or more years. Try to cut your time in college by getting college credits for doing well on Advanced Placement and College-level Examination Program tests. Think of ways you could cut your college budget such as used books, no car, limited social life, or cheaper living quarters.

Scholarships. Scholarships that you win become part of your financial aid package. They will not reduce your family contribution unless they exceed the amount of financial aid that you are offered. However, the more scholarships you receive, the less loan money you will have to repay.

If you find that you need more money after receiving your financial aid package, talk to the college about increasing your aid—it could happen. Many schools discover they have more money for aid because a number of students who were offered aid decide not to enroll in that college. When you need more money, you should also find out if the college or a local bank has any tuition budgeting plans or loan plans that could help you.

Guideposts to Financial Planning

Dreaming about going to college is fine, but obtaining the financial aid you need requires effort on your part. Make your aid seeking easier by following these guideposts:

- Begin your search for financial aid early in your senior year.

- Fill in all financial aid forms carefully.

- Apply as early as possible for all forms of financial aid.

- Take advantage of the help your parents, high school guidance or career counselors, and college financial aid counselors can give you.

Handling Acceptance and Rejection

13

Most students never have to handle rejection because 80 percent of all students are admitted to the college that they named as their first choice. The percentage of students being admitted to their first choice climbs even higher when those students who are applying to selective schools are not considered.

More than likely you will have the pleasant choice of deciding which college you will attend from several that have sent you acceptance notices. In this chapter, you will find out what to do if there are no acceptance notices in the mail and learn what a waiting list is and how to choose the college that you will attend.

What If You Are Rejected?

If your final list of colleges had some schools in the sure admissions category, you should have some acceptance letters even if you have a few rejections. It can be incredibly difficult to face your friends and family when you have not been admitted to your first- or even second-choice schools. Also, you may feel devastated and inclined to keep saying to yourself, "If only, I had done this or that." Perhaps it will help a little to know that most students after a few weeks at the college where they actually enroll wonder why it wasn't their first choice all along.

If you fail to be accepted at a Harvard, Yale, Stanford, or other equally selective school, remember that 80 to 85 percent of those who applied were also rejected and that the admissions officers of these schools admit that many who are rejected are capable of doing excellent work. Whether a student is rejected at a state-supported university or a very selective school, it is very important for him or her to handle rejection in a positive manner and to work for success at the school in which he or she enrolls.

The possibility of transferring

There is always the possibility of transferring to another college after attending a school for a year if you do not feel the school is the right one for you. You become an improved candidate for admission to a college that you applied to earlier if you have received good grades and demonstrated that you can handle college work. Admission as a transfer student is based more on college work than what students did in high school. It is far easier to transfer to a school where quite a few students drop out during their freshman year than to transfer to a very selective school that has few slots for transfer students.

Deciding to appeal rejection

Mistakes can be made. If you have all the qualifications for admission to a school, especially a state-supported school, and are rejected, you should ask for a review of your admissions file. Another reason for asking for a review is that you have done something after you applied that would make you a more attractive candidate for admission. This would mean doing things like improving your grades substantially during your senior year, really raising your SAT or ACT scores, or winning a very important award. Talk to your guidance counselor about whether or not you should appeal a rejection. Some colleges will admit a number of the students appealing rejection while others will rarely change an admissions decision.

Facing rejection from all colleges

Students usually receive all rejection notices when they have not carefully selected the colleges to which they apply. There are colleges within every state that will accept all high school graduates. These colleges usually have later deadlines for applications than more selective schools. So it is possible for most students, even at a late date, to find a college that will admit them. Students who have received rejections from all colleges should discuss with their parents and counselors how to find colleges that will not only admit them but meet their needs. They should also explore other options like waiting a year and applying to colleges again.

What If You Are Placed on a Waiting List?

Being placed on a waiting list means that the college will admit you if not enough students who were admitted decide to come to that college. Colleges want to have a full freshman class and will keep admitting students from the waiting list until they do so. At some schools, this can mean that students will not finally know whether they are accepted or rejected until very late in the summer.

What to do about being placed on a waiting list only matters if you truly want to attend that college. In that case, you should stay on the waiting list but at the same time accept a college which has admitted you because there is no guarantee that you will be accepted from the waiting list. You can call the college admissions office and find out what your chances of being admitted are. You also should write a letter to the college saying how much you still want to go to that college and giving any new information that might enhance your admissions prospects.

Choosing the College You Will Attend

More students than you might imagine have the problem of deciding which college they will attend, as many are admitted to more than one college. This can be a difficult decision with parents, teachers, and friends all pushing for different schools. The final decision must be the student's, and some time should be devoted to making it.

If you are in the position of having to decide which college you will attend, review the literature of the different colleges, then consider again the factors in chapter 10 that made you choose to apply to these colleges. Then rate each of these factors *excellent, good, average,* or *poor* for each college and assign an overall rating to each college. Most students will also have to add the factor of cost into their decision.

Selection Factors	Names of Colleges			
Location				
College environment				
Academic offerings and facilities				
Overall rating				

Considering the cost   All financial aid packages, even those for the same amounts, are not equal. Packages that offer more money in grants and scholarships are more attractive than those that offer more in loans. Use the cost considerations chart to compare costs of colleges that have admitted you.

Cost Considerations	Names of Colleges			
Total cost				
Financial aid offered				
Grants				
Loans				
Work-study				
Family contribution				

Once you have compared costs, you can visit or contact the financial aid offices at the different colleges to discuss your financial aid options.

Making your final decision

After you have been admitted to a college, many schools invite you to visit. Go if you can, stay in a dorm, visit classes, and wander around the school. There is no better way to test if a school feels right for you.

Then when you are back home, weigh all the factors and choose the school that seems to offer you most of the things that you want. If you can't seem to make up your mind because your choices seem so equal, then go with your feeling that a certain school is the right one for you. It is important to feel good about the college you will attend.

Completing the Admissions Process

Once you have made your final decision, send notification to the school that you accept its offer of admission along with all the other required paperwork. Be sure to notify the other schools that you will not be accepting their offers of admission so your place can go to another student. Finally, tell your counselor and the teachers who wrote recommendations for you where you will be attending college and thank them for their assistance in helping you be admitted to college.

APPENDIX A
Glossary

Achievement Tests are college admissions tests that measure students' knowledge or skills in different subjects.

ACT Assessment is one of the two major college admissions tests. The ACT has four tests: English, mathematics, reading, and science reasoning.

Advanced Placement Tests are tests that high school students take in order to gain college credit or placement in advanced courses at college.

Early action is an admissions option that lets students find out early if they have been accepted to a college but does not require a commitment to attend the school until the regular admissions acceptance deadline.

Early decision is an admissions option that gives early notification of acceptance and requires students to make a commitment to attend the admitting college.

Early evaluation is a plan that lets students find out early the likelihood of their being accepted to a college.

Family Financial Statement (FFS) is a form used to apply for financial aid from state and federal governments and colleges. Families fill in financial information that the American College Testing program uses to assess the amount of money a family should be able to contribute to a student's college education.

Financial Aid Form (FAF), like the FFS, is used to apply for financial aid from state and federal governments and colleges. After a family fills in financial information, the College Scholarship Service estimates what a family should be able to pay for a student's college expenses.

Ivy league schools are Brown, Columbia, Cornell, Dartmouth, Harvard, University of Pennsylvania, Princeton, and Yale. These selective schools were a sports league.

National Merit Scholarship is a scholarship that is awarded to students on the basis of scores on the PSAT/NMSQT and other factors.

P-ACT+ is a test that uses the same format as the ACT. It is normally taken by students in their sophomore year as a counseling tool.

Pell Grant is the largest federal grant program for undergraduates. It is a need-based grant that is awarded to all students who qualify.

Perkins Loans are federal loans that are administered by colleges. No interest is paid on these loans while students are in college.

Preliminary Scholastic Aptitude Test/National Merit Scholarship Qualifying Test (PSAT/NMSQT) is a multiple choice test composed of verbal and math sections like the SAT. Besides letting students see what the SAT is like, it is the qualifying test for the National Merit Scholarship program.

Rolling admissions is an admissions plan in which decisions about accepting or rejecting applicants are made by colleges shortly after receiving an application.

Scholastic Aptitude Test (SAT) is a college admissions test that has verbal and math sections and a test of standard written English. This test is required for admission to many colleges.

Stafford Student Loan is a guaranteed federal loan that allows students to borrow money from a bank or other lending agency. No interest is paid on the loan while students are attending school, and it is repaid at a government subsidized rate.

Supplemental Educational Opportunity Grant (SEOG) is a grant program of the federal government that is administered by colleges.

Test of Standard Written English (TSWE) is a 30-minute multiple choice test that is administered as part of the SAT.

Viewbook is a book or brochure with pictures that colleges put out to give prospective students information about the college.

Waiting list is a list of students who are neither accepted or rejected by a college but who will be accepted if students who were admitted decide not to attend the college.

Work-study program is a program in which college students work part-time at jobs while attending school. The program is funded by the federal government, state governments, and colleges.

APPENDIX B
Suggested
Reference Books

College Directories

College directories give you a quick overview of a number of colleges. They have information about admissions, costs, selectivity, student life, the college environment, and profiles of the freshman class for each college. You can find these directories in the library, career office, or guidance office at your high school and at public libraries and bookstores.

Barron's Profiles of American Colleges. Woodbury, New York: Barron's Education Series, Inc.

College Admissions Data Handbook. Concord, Massachusetts: Orchard House, Inc.

The College Handbook. New York: College Entrance Examination Board.

Comparative Guide to American Colleges. New York: Harper and Row Publishers.

Peterson's Guide to College Admissions. Princeton, New Jersey: Peterson's Guides.

Academic Programs and Majors

There are directories that will give you information about academic programs and majors at a large number of colleges. You will find these books in libraries.

Barron's Profiles of American Colleges, Index of College Majors. Woodbury, New York: Barron's Educational Series, Inc.

Index of Majors. New York: College Entrance Examination Board.

Financial Aid

Prospective college students should look at several books on financial aid because it is such a complex topic. You will find these books in libraries and bookstores.

Betterton, Don M. *How the Military Will Help You Pay for College.* Princeton, New Jersey: Peterson's Guides.

The College Cost Book. New York: College Entrance Examination Board.

Leider, Robert and Anna Leider. *Don't Miss Out.* New York: Simon and Schuster.

You can also get additional information by writing to these sources:

Need a Lift gives financial aid information that is especially helpful for students who are dependents of military personnel. Write to Emblem Sales, *Need a Lift*, Box 1050, Indianapolis, Indiana 46206. Include two dollars prepaid for the book.

Student Guide—Five Federal Financial Aid Programs describes five grant and loan programs for college students. Write to Federal Student Aid Programs, Department L-10, Pueblo, Colorado 81009 for a free copy.

Test Study Guides

These books, available at bookstores, are for students who want help in preparing for college admissions tests.

The College Board Achievement Tests. New York: College Entrance Examination Board. (actual tests)

How to Prepare for the SAT. Woodbury, New York: Barron's Educational Series, Inc.

Robinson, Adam and John Katzman. *The Princeton Review—The SAT and PSAT, Cracking the System.* New York: Villard Books.

10 SATs. New York: College Entrance Examination Board. (actual tests)

Other Helpful Books

These books are available at bookstores.

Bauld, Harry. *On Writing the College Application Essay.* New York: Barnes & Noble Books.

Gelband, Scott, Catherine Kubale, and Eric Schorr. *Your College Application.* New York: College Entrance Examination Board.

VGM CAREER BOOKS

CAREER DIRECTORIES
Careers Encyclopedia
Dictionary of Occupational Titles
Occupational Outlook Handbook

CAREERS FOR
Animal Lovers
Bookworms
Computer Buffs
Crafty People
Culture Lovers
Environmental Types
Film Buffs
Foreign Language Aficionados
Good Samaritans
Gourmets
History Buffs
Kids at Heart
Nature Lovers
Number Crunchers
Sports Nuts
Travel Buffs

CAREERS IN
Accounting; Advertising; Business; Child
Care; Communications; Computers;
Education; Engineering; Finance;
Government; Health Care; High Tech;
Law; Marketing; Medicine; Science;
Social & Rehabilitation Services

CAREER PLANNING
Beginning Entrepreneur
Career Planning & Development for
   College Students & Recent Graduates
Careers Checklists
Cover Letters They Don't Forget
Executive Job Search Strategies
Guide to Basic Resume Writing
Joyce Lain Kennedy's Career Book
Slam Dunk Resumes
Successful Interviewing for College
   Seniors

HOW TO
Approach an Advertising Agency and
   Walk Away with the Job You Want
Bounce Back Quickly After
   Losing Your Job
Change Your Career
Choose the Right Career
Get & Keep Your First Job
Get into the Right Law School
Get People to Do Things
   Your Way
Have a Winning Job Interview
Jump Start a Stalled Career
Land a Better Job
Launch Your Career in TV News
Make the Right Career Moves
Market Your College Degree
Move from College into a
   Secure Job
Negotiate the Raise
   You Deserve
Prepare a *Curriculum Vitae*
Prepare for College
Run Your Own Home Business
Succeed in College
Succeed in High School
Write Successful Cover Letters
Write a Winning Resume
Write Your College
   Application Essay

OPPORTUNITIES IN
Accounting
Acting
Advertising

Aerospace
Agriculture
Airline
Animal & Pet Care
Architecture
Automotive Service
Banking
Beauty Culture
Biological Sciences
Biotechnology
Book Publishing
Broadcasting
Building Construction Trades
Business Communication
Business Management
Cable Television
CAD/CAM
Carpentry
Chemistry
Child Care
Chiropractic
Civil Engineering
Cleaning Service
Commercial Art & Graphic Design
Computer Maintenance
Computer Science
Counseling & Development
Crafts
Culinary
Customer Service
Data Processing
Dental Care
Desktop Publishing
Direct Marketing
Drafting
Electrical Trades
Electronic & Electrical Engineering
Electronics
Energy
Engineering
Engineering Technology
Environmental
Eye Care
Fashion
Fast Food
Federal Government
Film
Financial
Fire Protection Services
Fitness
Food Services
Foreign Language
Forestry
Government Service
Health & Medical
High Tech
Home Economics
Homecare Services
Hospital Administration
Hotel & Motel Management
Human Resource Management
Information Systems
Installation & Repair
Insurance
Interior Design
International Business
Journalism
Laser Technology
Law
Law Enforcement & Criminal
   Justice
Library & Information Science
Machine Trades
Magazine Publishing
Marine & Maritime
Masonry
Marketing
Materials Science
Mechanical Engineering
Medical Imaging
Medical Technology

Metalworking
Military
Modeling
Music
Newspaper Publishing
Nonprofit Organizations
Nursing
Nutrition
Occupational Therapy
Office Occupations
Packaging Science
Paralegal
Paramedical
Part-time & Summer Jobs
Performing Arts
Petroleum
Pharmacy
Photography
Physical Therapy
Physician
Plastics
Plumbing & Pipe Fitting
Postal Service
Printing
Property Management
Psychology
Public Health
Public Relations
Purchasing
Real Estate
Recreation & Leisure
Refrigeration & Air Conditioning
Religious Service
Restaurant
Retailing
Robotics
Sales
Secretarial
Securities
Social Science
Social Work
Speech-Language Pathology
Sports & Athletics
Sports Medicine
State & Local Government
Teaching
Technical Writing &
   Communications
Telecommunications
Telemarketing
Television & Video
Theatrical Design & Production
Tool & Die
Transportation
Travel
Trucking
Veterinary Medicine
Visual Arts
Vocational & Technical
Warehousing
Waste Management
Welding
Word Processing
Writing
Your Own Service Business

RESUMES FOR
Advertising Careers
Banking and Financial Careers
College Students &
   Recent Graduates
Communications Careers
Education Careers
Engineering Careers
Environmental Careers
Health and Medical Careers
High School Graduates
High Tech Careers
Midcareer Job Changes
Sales and Marketing Careers
Scientific and Technical Careers

VGM Career Horizons
a division of *NTC Publishing Group*
4255 West Touhy Avenue
Lincolnwood, Illinois 60646-1975